Bobby

THE
MIDNIGHT HOUR

Brother we got a long way to go

Scoot

JIMMY DREW

THE
MIDNIGHT HOUR

AN AMAZING JOURNEY FROM PARALYSIS

TATE PUBLISHING
AND ENTERPRISES, LLC

Published by Tate Publishing & Enterprises, LLC
127 E. Trade Center Terrace | Mustang, Oklahoma 73064 USA
1.888.361.9473 | www.tatepublishing.com

Tate Publishing is committed to excellence in the publishing industry. The company reflects the philosophy established by the founders, based on Psalm 68:11,
"The Lord gave the word and great was the company of those who published it."

Published in the United States of America

ISBN: 978-1-62746-728-5
1. Biography & Autobiography / Personal Memoirs
2. Biography & Autobiography / General
13.12.02

DEDICATION

So many people have been there for me at one point or the other. My precious mother never gave up on me and it is to her I dedicate this book. She slept in a hospital waiting room for 8 weeks waiting on me, when everyone else presumed me dead. She fought with doctors who wanted to remove my life support because she knew I would not give up. For that and all her many prayers that have been lifted up for me since, I am eternally grateful. There are so many people I owe a special thanks to and I truly wish there were enough pages to include them all. Mike "Cooter" Kirkindoll has been an unbelievable friend. If I were to call Coot and say send money; most people would ask why. Cooter would only ask how much. He has been there for me more times than I can remember. Mike "Bubba" White has been the single most important person in my life. There will be much rejoicing in heaven because of what he did for me. There may be one very confused pizza man. Vance Hale, keep practicing on that gill; believe me brother you need it. I love you and your barbeque. Mostly I love you and thanks for the ending. Most of all thanks to Amy Kay. Amy is the reason I am about to take my next breath. Someday Sweet Amy there will be peace in the valley for both of us. I will always love you.

CONTENTS

HOT ROD AND
A ROCK WALL

We had sporadically driven Jeb's Honda Civic down just about every twisting back road within a fifty-mile circumference of Winnsboro, Texas, that night. Those East Texas blacktops seemed to be laid out for driving and partying, and we were putting them to good use. I was so drunk that I couldn't have staggered home with two sober friends supporting me, much less have safely driven my car. Jeb had just arrived home from the Marine Corps boot camp without graduating because a knee injury. The same knee injury remarkably healed itself as soon as Jeb was away from the rigors of boot camp. As soon as my senior year was over, the marines were going to kick the crap out of me too, but there would be no quitting. With every shot of whiskey or toke off a joint, we gave each other a hearty "Semper Fi."

When Jeb pulled up beside my car and told me to get out, I looked at him like he were joking and said, "Man, there is no way I can drive."

The look on his face told me this was not a joke, so I pleaded, "Please give me a ride home."

Jeb said, "No, man, you can make it."

Holding up a nearly empty bottle of Southern Comfort, I pleaded, "Look at this."

Adding to it, I said, "I've had just as much beer as you have too."

Jeb looked over his shoulder into the back at Stephanie and said, "Get out, man, you can make it."

Desperately, I looked at Stephanie and said, "Please help me. There is no way I can make it!"

Even though she looked concerned, Stephanie shrugged her shoulders and asked, "What can I do?"

By this time, the thought of my friend forcing me to drive crazy drunk had me so mad that throwing the door open, I struggled to my feet. Wobbling there frozen in time, the surety of inebriation was not with me at all. The chances of me making it home in my rocket-powered Nova were slim and none. Just before shutting Jeb's door, I leaned in and looked at him and said, "You little weasel, if anything happens to me, it is on your head."

Then I slammed his door with as much force as my drunken state would allow. It was only two miles to my house, and after all, what could happen in two miles? After getting into my car, the fear subsided, and the effect of the alcohol finally gave me a false sense of security. When that engine fired up, the rocking rumble and the headers popping gave me a sense of pride. With all the primer on it, my hot rod did not look like much, but it would smoke the tires going into second gear. As my car fishtailed out of that parking lot, my rebel yell could have been heard from blocks away.

I flew by the police station at around eighty miles an hour with the windows down blasting AC/DC. Two hundred yards past the police station were the tracks. It seems like every Norman Rockwall–like small town in America has railroad tracks running through the city limits. These tracks turned to the country and passed two hundred yards behind my house. Twice a day a mile-long coal train would pass behind my house with the engineer blowing that lonesome whistle.

Riding the breaks took my miles per hour down to thirty, and the tracks jostled one of the paint cans in the backseat to the floor. Assured by the thud, there was no reason to look back; it was just a good thing that the seal on the can had not been broken. At the light, sharply turning the wheel to the right and pinning the accelerator to the floor, my car launched out of the hole like Apollo XIII on its ill-fated mission.

With the frustration and disappointment of one bad choice after another heavy on my mind, my foot was trying to push a hole through the floor with the accelerator. The road from the intersection of Main Street and Broadway to my house is relatively straight with one exception. Broadway runs right through the geographical center of the sleepy, little town of Winnsboro. Placing a twenty-five-mile-per-hour curve on a main thoroughfare in the center of town was totally uncalled for. At that inappropriately placed curve, the road wound around a small wood-frame house that sat on top of a hill. There was a rock wall at the edge of the road that served as a retaining wall for that hill. The rocks in that wall looked as though they had been placed there at the beginning of time.

As the needle of my speedometer passed one hundred and ten miles an hour, a sickening revelation fell upon me. There was no way I could drive that heavy hot rod through that twenty-five mile-per-hour curve going that fast on a rain-slick road. The curl of the street was to my left, and upon entering its hook, my car lurched into a power slide. Experience told me to slightly turn the wheel toward the slide, but at that speed, it was too late, and gravity told me something else. At that moment, my life was in God's hands, and the way I had been living my life, that was not where I wanted to be.

The right rear tire of my supercharged Nova swung around and hit the four-inch curb at the apex of that curve. When that tire and wheel hit that curb, it sent my car flying end over end across the street like a Tomahawk cruise missile. The tires on the back were street-slick fifties and the rear end was jacked up with air shocks to keep the rubber from rubbing. Dale Earnhardt Jr. could not have brought that car out of that slide, but then he would not have gone into it. The trunk slammed into that wall, and my body shot through the back glass like a bullet from a high-powered rifle. The last conscious memory that I have of that night was my head popping down onto my shoulders like a medicine ball dropped from a third-floor window.

The inertia built up in the car catapulted it over that wall, somersaulting it into the top of a cedar tree in the front yard of that house. The elasticity of the evergreen tree shot my car back into the street like a pinball just before a tilt. All this time, that gallon of metallic-blue paint and another gallon of thinner was flying around inside that car bouncing off me like lottery balls bouncing around a hopper. I had been working on restoring this car for months and was going to paint it the next morning. With my good friends Jerry White and Albert Lopez helping, we had replaced everything from the motor to the exhaust. The old bench seat had been replaced with bucket seats that, for some reason, did not seem to warrant seat belts.

Immediately after my car came to a stop, I was looking down at the wreckage and knew this could not be good at all. There were people coming out of their houses and running frantically in the direction my car. Even though it was obvious to see they were yelling at each other, their voices were muffled and could not be heard. There was a police car that arrived at the scene of the accident with its lights on, but the siren could not be heard either.

At that point, there was a feeling that this evil, sinister, wicked presence was behind me and waiting to snatch my soul away from this world and deliver it to hell. Just like that, my life had gone to another side that until that moment, there were serious doubts in my mind of its existence. My eyes were transfixed on the wreck knowing full well if the God that I ignored so proudly did not give me a second chance, whatever was behind me was going to drag me kicking and screaming to hell. This was not just an awareness that I was in the presence of evil, but I also felt the very hands of the devil around my throat, squeezing the soul from my body.

There was an apartment complex close, and there were a lot of people coming outside to see what had happened. They were people who knew me and knew the sound that my big hot rod made. There were a few people praying in a small circle with hands grasped to each other much the same way my soul held grasp to a dead body. My mother and my grandmother had exposed me to religion all my life. Then to me religion was a crutch for weak people, and this old boy was anything but weak.

As soon as that circle formed and my friends started praying for me, the foolishness of my thinking became so apparent. Standing at the edge of life and death and knowing beyond certainty that there was something after life was terrifying. My life had been cloaked in absolute dualism for the sake of whatever company happened to be around at that time. In a moment's notice, wings would pop out of my snuff can, and there was an angel at your beckon call. The next moment, a fifth of Jim Beam would fly out of that same snuff can, and the party was on.

When the ambulance arrived, there was some confusion among the emergency medical technicians. The smell of the paint and thinner was so strong in the air that they believed the car was about to blow up. Everyone was urging them to get me out of the wrecked car, but they did not have a death wish. Finally, my friend Peter Chris went in through the windshield and pulled me out. Courage is not the absence of fear, because my friend was afraid. Courage is facing your fear and doing that which you were afraid to do in the first place. The story that I am about to tell you would not be a story to tell if it were not for Peter pulling me out of that car.

Knowing there were demons all around me waiting to take me to eternal torment, my eyes were transfixed on my corpse. Somehow it was obvious to me that if my eyes drifted from that lifeless, bloody, blue form lying on the street, there would be no second chance. There was no tunnel with a light at the end drawing me toward it or a man in a flowing, white robe. There was only the realization that my life had been a disastrous waste. After Peter pulled me out, the ambulance personnel jumped into action just like the heros they always wanted to be. Later they sent my dad a letter telling him they were going to sue if he did not pay for their uniforms the blue paint ruined. More about my dad later and you'll see they came as close to death as me.

After my body was placed in the ambulance, the emergency medical technicians went to work with everything; they had sopping blue paint off it. The hospital was only a short mile away, and on a cold and rainy February night, the only traffic were my friends who were racing to the emergency room. The ambulance arrived at the hospital with several carloads of my friends in tow and more arriving each second. My family doctor who had known me since we had moved to Winnsboro in the third grade had been called to come in to the hospital. Dr. Murley had a son who was my age and was very well acquainted with me.

Everyone in the emergency room had watched me grow up, and it was a hard thing to conduct business as usual because of knowing me personally. When they wheeled me into the hospital emergency room, there were no vital signs, and they were uncertain how long my brain had been without oxygen. A team of three nurses and Dr. Murley worked to restore my heartbeat and breathing, even though they were swimming in a sea of blue paint. Everything that came into contact with me was coated with paint.

By this time, there were around twenty friends in the waiting room all sitting on the floor holding hands and praying. Jeb and

Stephanie had been at the scene of the accident but were not in the emergency room. Later, Stephanie told me Jeb was afraid that somehow he would go to jail for getting me drunk and had been scared to be there. It was over twenty years later before it came back to me, and I asked her for the truth. My best friend was there, and though he had never shown any sign of a religious bone in his body, he was fervently calling out to God.

Back in the emergency room, the minute hand on the clock was moving much faster than usual. Using almost every available gauze pad and dressing, the staff managed to remove enough paint from my chest to make contact with a defibrillator. After twenty minutes on the operating table in the emergency room, a nurse pleaded, "Dr. Murley, he is gone."

Dr. Murley looked at her and said, "Work with me or get out."

Then he rubbed the mallets for friction and yelled, "Contact!"

I had been watching everything that went on in the emergency room and alternating to the waiting room as well. Every prayer that was being lifted up, and every blue medical instrument was under my scrutiny. The evil was right there beside me the whole time, lingering in the shadows, waiting to escort me to my new home. When Dr. David Murley hit me that last time, I heard a heart monitor beep, and everything went black, and my body slipped into a coma.

LIGHTS OUT

My coma lasted for eight weeks and was spent drifting like an untethered balloon bouncing off any structure that got in it way. Breathing machines and feeding tubes kept me alive in this deep state of unconsciousness when the body is unresponsive to external stimuli. My comatose nap lasted for eight weeks, and there are dangers of patients on breathing machines for over thirty days never resuming breathing on their own. Doctors kept me on a ventilator for four weeks after waking from my coma.

On the day that my coma broke, a young nurse beside my bed was taking care of me. My short-term memory was gone, and these surroundings did not look at all familiar to me, and I was thinking how in the world I got here. Paralysis kept me from moving any part of my body or even turning my head.

I could see that nurse out of my peripheral vision, so I tried to ask her where I was. Not a sound came out of my mouth, so I swallowed and tried again. Panic hit me like a monster had me by the ankle and was pulling me underwater. Wanting to scream, I gasped for air and attempted another try at vocalization. There is no cage that is nearly as confining as being locked inside your own mind, and like a man drowning in quicksand, my breathing was hurried and panicked.

So many thoughts and emotions were racing through my head as I lay there unable to move or communicate them to anyone in any way. A sudden avalanche of emotion flooded my heart, and tears exploded from my eyes like a virtual rainstorm. All of the time I had been in a coma, oils had built up in my body, and like water running to the low spot, as the tears flowed so flowed the oil. All of the sudden, things had gone from very bad to unimaginable because my eyes were burning like hot coals. Now not only could I not move or talk, but my eyes were also in excruciating pain. I was in such pain from the tears of fire that it made me forget about the nurse beside me, but she had noticed me. I saw her lean down and hover over me she looked into my eyes, and then I heard her say, "Oh my God, Jimmy is crying."

A large man came over and looked at my tear-stained eyes and, after putting a hand on my shoulder, said, "I'll go get his mother."

Until then the gravity of the situation had not allowed to focus on anything but that exact moment. Upon hearing that tender name on which the world turns, in my mind I screamed, *Mom, where are you? Please come and take me home.*

Another nurse who was standing there put something on gauze and began to blot my eyes with it. Whatever this angel of mercy was doing did not take all of the pain away, but it did help and would become my best friend because the tears were always there. I was a young man so lost on the wrong side of the tracks of life and death that even his tears caused pain.

On the night of my accident at about midnight, my parents were getting ready for bed when there was a knock at the door. My dad went to the door and saw the pastor of our church standing there, crying. He turned and said, "Betty, get some clothes on."

Mom came walking out of the bedroom and asked, "What is it?"

Then she saw Pastor Boyd Day standing there crying, and she knew.

Pastor Day told my dad when they went to the hospital to take FM 515 so that they would not pass by the scene of my accident. Dad had known this could happen any day and had had prepared himself for it in a way. Mom had just been in denial that anything bad could happen to her alcoholic, drug-addicted son. Dad's answer was to fight me harder and to be a stricter enforcer of the already-novel length list of rules he had for me. Mom's answer was to just pray about it and expect God to take care of it.

Mom had been to a revival meeting at her church that night, and a young evangelist had stopped mid-sermon and asked Mom if he could pray for her. That young man told Mom that something was about to happen in her life that would take every ounce of faith she had to get through. Mom left church that night with me on her mind.

At the emergency room, people who had watched me grow up were fighting against overwhelming odds to save my life. Slamming into a rock wall with my head laid it open like a watermelon that had been dropped from a two-story window. Dr. Murley knew one thing: the emergency room at the hospital in Winnsboro was not equipped to treat injuries like the ones I had sustained. The one thing that really stacked the odds against the emergency room staff was the blue paint. It covered me totally and was all over everything that came in contact with me. There was no way they could follow normal procedure for dealing with my injuries.

They were preparing to transfer me to the hospital in Tyler by the time Mom and Dad walked into the hospital waiting room. By the time my parents got there, the waiting room was full of my friends. The word was, they brought me into the hospital with no vital signs and were working to restore them. Immediately John Lopez, trying to hold back his own tears, came to my parents and embraced my mother. The summer before my senior year, I had lived with John and his sons. Although John did not have claim to being my father, he loved me just like he did Ricky and Albert.

About that time, Dr. Murley walked into the waiting room covered in blue paint and blood. My friends all rushed to surround him to get news on the status of my condition. They all wanted to know if their life long friend was going to live.

John told them, "Y'all get back and let the doctor speak to Jim and Betty."

My dad asked, "Is he alive?"

Dr. Murley said, "We restored his vital signs."

Mom took her first full breath of air after receiving the news and exclaimed, "Praise God."

There was a collective sigh of relief from everyone in the waiting room. Charles Carson was trying to be strong for my parents, but on the inside, he was crumbling down. He knew the toll that the alcohol and drugs were taking on me and the hopelessness that drove me to abuse them in the first place. Charles and I had recently been in a fight, and I had said some really bad things to him. We had not spoken to each other in a couple of weeks, and I can't imagine the way my best friend was feeling.

Charles walked up to Mom and embraced her as he told her, "If anyone can do this, Hoot can."

That was all that my best friend ever called me. *Hoot* was short for *Hooter*, which was a derivative of *Scooter*.

My dad saw this look on Dr. Murley's face that led him to believe everything was not all right, so he asked, "What are you not telling us?"

Dr. Murley wiped the sweat from his brow and dropped his gaze to the floor and said, "Scooter's brain was without oxygen for so long. If he lives, it will be in a vegetative state."

Then he said, "We are transporting him to Tyler now."

Jerry White looked at Charles and said, "Let's go!"

John looked at Jerry and told him, "Go by the house and pick up Albert and Ricky."

My friends drove to Tyler while swimming in a turbulent sea of emotion unable to control a torrent of tears. Although he was in a frantic state, Jerry drove with the flashers on at over one hundred miles an hour. They were pulled over by a highway patrolman right outside of Tyler. After the officer came to the driver's window of Jerry's car and saw them crying, he asked, "What is the emergency?"

Sobbing uncontrollably, Jerry told him, "Our brother has been in a very bad accident and is at the Tyler hospital."

Then Albert added, "We got to get there before he dies."

Seeing the genuine grief on their faces, the trooper said, "Turn your flashers off and follow me."

He turned to go back to his car but stopped and, turning back, said, "Stay right behind me."

At high speeds, he led them to the hospital through red lights with cars pulling over out of the way.

Even the trauma unit at the much larger hospital in Tyler was not equipped to handle the injuries that my body had sustained. Within just a few hours, they transported me to Galveston by ambulance because care flight would have been a waste. My parents and friends were told not to make the trip to John Sealy because there was no way they would get me there alive.

When my mother arrived at my bedside, my tears stopped and my anguished expression faded into a smile. The man who had gone to get Mom was a respiratory therapist named Bill Watts. Bill saw my smile and said, "Look, he recognizes his mother."

My neurosurgeon, Dr. Donovan, said, "That is not possible."

Mom said, "My baby is awake."

I rolled my eyes toward my mother and tried to say, "Momma."

I did not make a sound, but everyone knew what I was trying to say. Bill looked at Dr. Donovan and said, "He knows."

Dr. Donovan said, "I don't understand."

He went on, pointing out, "With all the time his brain was without oxygen, there is no way he has remaining brain function."

Mom had been in Galveston sleeping in the waiting room the whole eight weeks that I had been in my coma. She had an apartment, but the only time she ever went there was to take a shower and maybe take a quick nap. Even though doctors told her I would not come out of the coma, she knew that her God was bigger than any coma. She was going to be there by my side when I woke up and not in some apartment on the other side of town.

After the car accident before they could really do anything for me other than stabilize my condition, they had to try and get the paint off. For years after the accident, there were scars on me where the paint thinner they used to get that blue paint off of my body burned me. They stopped just short of taking sandpaper and stripping the paint off like I was an antique table found at a rummage sale.

My neck was broken at the third cervical vertebra, which at that time was a very high break to even live. The only thing I had going for me in this time of great uncertainty was that the break was incomplete. By incomplete I mean that the spinal cord was not completely severed. The spinal cord runs through the spinal column and extends from the base of the skull downward to the small of the back. Every single thing that takes place in the body is dependent upon both ascending and descending impulses in the spinal cord. The nerves communicate with the spinal cord by electrical impulses that are carried along by neurons. Each neuron fires and discharges an electric impulse that travels across a microscopic gap to the next neuron. This exchange of electric impulses between two neurons is called a synaptic connection.

There are multiplied billions of these synaptic connections in each movement. Any break in the cord, depending on the location of the injury, results in loss of function to specific areas of the body. Any injury to the spinal cord located at or below C5 results in quadriplegia, or affecting all four limbs. No two spinal cord injuries are the same because of the amount of damage done to the spinal cord. There are those lucky few who have broken their neck and got up and walked away from it believing they had superhuman strength. Good fortune and strength should never be misconstrued, especially when a blessing is involved.

I was an eighteen-year-old boy who thought he had the world in the palm of his hands, when in reality, the world had me in the palm of its hands. I thought that I was ten-foot tall and bulletproof and could leap tall buildings in a single bound. Now I was paralyzed from the neck down and could not talk or communicate in any way, and the simplest of tasks was forgotten to me. The only thing I could do on my own was cry, and that caused a great deal of pain, so much so that I began to get so anxious when I started to get emotional, and I was always emotional. Living in my mind was the only thing that kept me going. I've always heard that it is not good to live in the past, but the past was all that I had.

WILD ROOTS

I would not have traded growing up in the country for all the city streets in the world. The old country farmhouse that we moved into was two miles outside of Winnsboro, Texas, on Highway 11. We moved there from Longview, Texas, the summer between third- and fourth-grade in school. Going from a city with a population of 74,000 to a small town of 3,400 was a culture shock for a nine-year-old boy. We moved from a city of Cub Scout dens to a modern-day episode of *The Waltons*. Strangely enough, on the half-mile stretch of highway where our house sat, there were a lot of other kids to play with. I had never fished in a pond before we moved to the country. My father was an avid fisherman and took me every time he went, but that was always from a boat and normally at lakes larger than Winnsboro. There were six good fishing ponds within walking distance from my house, so learning to pond fish was a necessity.

There was a mixture of evergreen trees and oaks that seemed to touch the sky in Wood County. Hay fields rolled along the sides of the highways like floating cumulus clouds in the heavens. There were miles and miles of blacktop roads teaming with game. There were places on these roads where the trees were so thick you could not see past the barbwire fence. In other stretches, there were cattle pastures with big, red barns and John Deere tractors.

The big country farmhouse that we moved into had been built by my grandfather. My father built houses for a living as well until he tried his hand at farming. He always did some framing jobs on the side though. Dad always said he was the greatest carpenter since Jesus Christ. It was really a good thing that he was a great carpenter because farming was not his forte. He never really went as far as trying to make a living by any crops we grew, and to this day, I am convinced he did it to keep me busy and out of trouble.

It was surprising that in a mile-long stretch of highway where I lived, there were so many kids to do things with. I was the youngest by a few years and took it on the chin a lot at first. Once there was about fifteen kids gathered up in this lot playing a game of football. We were playing tackle, and I was getting tackled every play, whether I had the ball or not. They were going to push it as far as they could take it; or rather, I would let them. This man who lived in the house next door to the lot where we played came home from work and came to my rescue.

Harpo was a pipeline welder and drove a big, blue welding truck with a grill on the back that he personally made. As he pulled into his driveway, we could hear ZZ Top thumping "I'm Bad, I'm Nationwide" even with his windows up. Harpo was a big, muscular man with a full beard. He was the kind of guy you would want to see walk around the corner if you were in some kind of trouble. He had a strong reputation of being a man you did not want to have any trouble with.

He sat in his truck and rolled a smoke and watched all those other kids having so much fun abusing me. Stanley was not hard to get along with when he was by himself. He lived in the house next door with his younger brother and three younger sisters. Even though he was five years older than me, we had a lot of fun most of the time. Mike was a year younger than Stanley, but when he was around, the two of them terrorized me. Even when

Stanly was on my team, he would lay me out on passes so they could flatten me.

Everyone around the neighborhood looked up to Harpo, so when we saw him walking over, we stopped playing and ran to him. Harpo has a smile that you have to see to appreciate. He was walking over to the lot where we were playing smiling like the Cheshire cat.

As he stepped onto the lot, he announced, "I want to play."

Stanley called out, "We got Harpo!"

Harpo looked at him coldly and said, "Me and Scooter against all of you."

I had yet to see my first *Cheech & Chong* movie, so it took me a few years to understand his smile when he said, "We will let them kick off."

They lined up on the other end of the lot and threw me the ball, the sandlot equivalent of a kickoff. Harpo stepped close, and I tried to hand him the ball, but turning, he looked at them and said, "Follow me."

I looked like a water bug bouncing around that field following my lead blocker. He made it a point to knock them all down at least once before allowing me to score. When we kicked off, Harpo broke through their wedge, and I was able to bring the return man down. Besides me, there were fourteen kids playing ranging from seventh grade to the twelfth. They were rough on me, but with Harpo backing me up, I could be rough right back. Mike even told me, "Harpo is not always going to be around."

Harpo, in turn, told Mike, "He knows he can get me any time he needs me."

Then he looked at me and said, "Don't be scared."

I was in the fourth grade, and Harpo and I won the game in all the glory of the Super Bowl itself. After that game and up to this day, I call him Uncle Harpo.

Being a farm boy meant there was always hard work readily available and plenty of it. We never had that many animals, but Dad insisted on growing the feed for the few pigs and cows that we did own. The home-grown feed consisted of five acres of peanuts and five acres of corn. We did not have any farmhands or a combine to gather and process that acreage. My dad had a red-headed stepchild who worked for the all home cooking he could get. My dad married my mother when I was only seven, and the discipline thing did not go over to well at first. He soon learned that beating me did not work nearly as well as hard labor and did not serve a purpose other than wasting his time.

There were summer days when I lured the neighborhood kids to the pea patch with promises of cool watermelon and swimming in the coldest spring-fed lake in the county. It was not easy being a modern-day Tom Sawyer because there were not any fences to whitewash. If you can get your friends into the pea patch in the sweltering summer heat, you have pulled the ultimate con.

The gift of persuasion was always easy for me, and it was a talent that I learned to make good use of. It got me elected class president my junior year in high school and nominated my senior year. Our senior class sponsor was Mrs. Gladys Burkham, and the road to the graduation podium at Winnsboro High School ran through her senior English class. As soon as I was nominated for office in our first senior class meeting, she made it perfectly clear that she would not be working with me. There had been a little mishap my junior year involving the misappropriation of funds.

Totally on my own, I did this fund-raising car wash thing on the weekends to raise money for the junior-senior prom. I washed and waxed cars for twenty dollars apiece. When I was a junior, the minimum wage was four dollars and twenty-five cents an hour. Normally it took me about an hour to do a car unless it was Coach Clark's corvette or Coach Hawkins's RX7. They took about forty-five minutes and then about an hour and a half of cruising. In a normal week, I would do four or five cars so there was some good money coming in from my fund-raising efforts.

As the prom approached, our class sponsor asked me for all of the money I had raised. When I told her it all went to expenses, she had a problem with the figures. Besides the numbers not looking right, she did not think that cold beer and marijuana constituted a legitimate expense. She called a special class meeting and called for an impeachment vote. As I was leaving the room, Charles Carson yelled, "Don't worry, Scooter, you'll still be president when you get back!"

It takes a two-thirds majority vote to impeach a standing president, and as president of the parliamentary procedure team, I pointed that out before leaving the room. I felt sorry for our sponsor in a way, because not one person voted for impeachment. My friends would follow me anywhere, especially into trouble.

All my life, my thinking told me there would be plenty of time to have all the fun that a life of sin would allow before settling down. There was never a time in my short life when the certainty of the existence of God existed in me. In my selfish little world, there was even a brief period when the world only existed in my mind and I was the only actual live human being. With me being the center of the universe, there was never a reason to live for God. Religion was for old people and the weak, and until now, I was neither of those.

FROM DEATH TO LIFE

With my back against the wall, I knew it was time to let go of my foolish pride and ask Jesus into my heart. Religion was always shoved down my throat from the time of my early childhood. I knew both what to do and what you say and had even stumbled through those steps more than once as a child. My grandmother told me that a profession of faith and asking Jesus into your heart had to be done with repentance, or it did not mean anything. Going down to a church and praying some form prayer does not prepare you for what you face when your soul leaves your dead body. The life that you lead after that prayer is what gets you past the demons that so desperately want to trade you an eternity of torment for your life of disobedience.

The only thing that would come to my remembrance about my accident was the evil presence that engulfed me. After that experience, it was clear that the love of God was not just a crutch for the old and the weak after all. There were stories in the Bible that had been repeated to me many times during my childhood about Jesus performing miracles. There were even people in the Bible that had even been raised from the dead, and in my young mind, God was my answer. Though audibly I could not pray because of paralyzed vocal cords, in my mind and in my heart I prayed with every ounce of courage left in my weak body. I asked God to forgive me of my sins and come into my heart and save me. There was never a more serious prayer for salvation at any time or any place. How could someone who had never experienced the evil that awaits the unrepentant sinners of this world on the other side fully appreciate the saving grace of Jesus?

The staff at John Sealy all took to me magically. No one came by and wheeled my bed down to the cafeteria for coffee and doughnuts in the morning or tea and crumpets in the afternoon. It was just a kind word here and there or stopping by for a couple of minutes to talk before going home at the end of a shift. For the last eight weeks, the emergency room staff had been hearing stories from my friends about me before the accident. Even though I ended up in a hospital four hundred miles from Winnsboro, there were a steady flow of my friends visiting. They knew there was something special about me to have all those friends driving so far to see me, when I would not even know they had been there.

The break in my neck required an operation in which a piece of bone was taken from my hip and fused with the third and fourth vertebrae. There are eight centimeters of surgical wire wrapped around the bone fusion in my neck like a figure eight. Back in 1983, people with injuries like the ones I had sustained did not live, and they did not think about making a recovery. At that time, the only person that I had in my life who did not give up on me was my precious mother. After what she had already been through with the loss of my sister, there was no way she could take the death of another child.

When I was a five years old, we lived in Dallas on Ewing Street in the Oak Cliff area of Dallas. One day, my two older sisters and I were in the backyard playing with a ball. Debbie was five years older than me, and Jamie was three years older. Jamie took great joy in tormenting her little brother to the point of tears at least once a day. Our house sat on a corner lot in a nice, quiet neighborhood in the heart of Dallas in a time when people could go to sleep with only their screen doors closed. Debbie kicked the ball between me and Jamie, and it rolled out into the street. Clumsily I turned to run out and get the ball, but Jamie grabbed me by the wrist and pulled me into a sitting position and ran after the ball.

This was long before there were any laws against drinking and driving or the existence of the organization MADD. The lady driving the car that hit and killed my sister was so drunk she could not stand up. I was so young when this happened that the only clear memory that I have of it is my father in the street on his knees with my sister's lifeless body in his arms. He was screaming at the top of his lungs, and on the inside, that screaming never stopped.

There are two types of people when it comes to the way they handle adversity when it comes. There are those who will fight through adversity and grow stronger for the experience. Some people take trouble when it comes as a reason to give up on life, and they forget the people who love and depend on them. That is what my biological father did. He forgot his responsibility to his other two children and wife, and he slowly but methodically killed himself with booze and pills. By the time I was seven, Mom had remarried my stepfather. Until then she worked waitress jobs and did whatever she had to do to take care of me and Debbie. She fought through losing one child and resolved not to do it again.

Bill was the very first real friend that I made at John Sealy, and he taught me so much about what determination could do for a person when they are down. One of the worst things about a break as high as mine are the respiratory problems that come with being a quadriplegic. Complete and incomplete spinal cord injuries cause serious respiratory problems. I had a tracheotomy, and all throughout the night, people from respiratory would come in to clean my trachea. All through the day and night, respiratory therapist like my friend Bill would clean the tracheal tube in my throat.

My speech pathologist showed up at my bed one day with something in her hand called a communication board. It had the letters of the alphabet on it and simple words like *yes* and *no*. The way it worked was you spelled out words by blinking your eyes when the person holding the board pointed to letters. Until then my communication was limited to one blink for *yes* and two blinks for *no*. The very first thing I spelled out was, "You are cute."

My beautiful, new friend laughed and said, "You are cute too."

Next, we spelled, "Get me out of here."

Curiously she asked, "Why?"

Then we spelled, "Sad here."

As an eighteen-year-old boy, it was not hard to understand the gravity of my situation. What was hard for me to deal with were all of the people who were dying around me. The only thing that really worked the same on me were my ears, and the sounds of death were all around. Like a young soldier who was laid out on the ground with his comrades dying all around him, I prayed to be somewhere else.

The very next day, I was moved onto a private room, and I met the people who would take care of me for the next six months. These are people who after thirty years, I still remember their names and faces and the wonderful way they treated me. Spiritually they may not have actually been angels, but they always have been to me.

The head nurse on the ninth floor was a tall, feisty brunette named Barbara Turner. She was my saving grace as the months rolled by and time became my biggest enemy. I remembered watching my favorite movie star in the movie *Midway* starring John Wayne growing up. The Duke played a naval officer who was paralyzed in a naval battle and was placed in a hospital bed to live with his paralysis. Being a man of the highest fortitude and of rock-solid character, he did not accept that bed as his final sentence. He lay there staring at his paralyzed feet repeating the same words out loud over and over.

He would say with determination that only the duke could muster, "Going to move that toe."

Then he would repeat with the same fervor, "Going to move that toe."

After some time, he moved it and made a recovery, and that was just what I resolved within myself to do. I would lay there in my bed trying so hard to move that people would walk into my room and mistake my facial contortions for pain. Mom would tell them, "He is just trying to move."

My first movement was a twitch in my left index finger, and it was like a shot of adrenaline to my spirit. After that first movement in my finger, there was no holding me back. Within two weeks, I was able to use that finger to press the nurse-call button, and Mom finally felt easy enough to go back home.

My dad and my aunt and uncle drove down to bring Mom back home from the hospital. It was hard for Mom to leave me there by myself. In the days leading up to her going home, she must have asked everyone from the chief of staff to the housekeepers to keep an eye on me.

The day my dad arrived, he walked into my room and took out his big Buck pocketknife and said, "I bet I can get those feet to move."

He flipped open the blade and gently touched it to the bottom of my left foot. The tickle created a reflex called a flexor withdrawal. My knee snapped up like I was a high-stepping Aggie Drum Major.

Dad said, "Son, I'll have the tractor gassed up."

Trying not to cry, he pleaded, "Hurry home."

I was too excited over my first movement in my leg to be sad when I was left there alone. I knew Mom could not stay there with me forever, and it really would be good for me not to depend on her. A few nights before she left, we were having trouble communicating what I needed, and we both started to cry. When Mom started to cry, she went into the bathroom to be alone. I could hear her praying and asking God to help me. She stayed in the bathroom for a long time, sobbing and praying, and I was really worried about her. Pressing the nurse-call button, I had to get a nurse to check on her.

By reading my lips, one of the nurses figured out that Mom was in the bathroom, and I wanted her to see about her. When Kathy came out, her face was sullen, and she said, "Betty just needs some time alone."

In a scratchy but clearly audible voice, I said, "Thank you."

Throwing open the bathroom door, Kathy screamed, "Betty, he is talking!"

Mom came dashing out of the bathroom, and my first words to her were, "I love you."

Now she could leave me in peace.

The day after Mom had gone home, my physical therapist, Adele Walker, came walking in and said, "Boy, I hear they can't shut you up."

They had long since removed my halo brace, and I turned my head to look at my friend and said, "I don't sound very good."

Adele said, "We can understand you."

Placing a hand on top of my head, she said, "You are the talk of this hospital."

Inquisitively I asked, "Why?"

She smiled and said, "People here love you because you are a fighter."

Then Adele said, "You have been here a long time, blue boy."

That was how everyone referred to me as when they first brought me into John Sealy Hospital. Most of the paint that covered me had to wear off, and that took some time because of me being so still. It was a big deal when I came in, not because of the severity of my injuries, but because I was Scooter Smurf—the first person to ever come in that huge hospital painted blue, or any other color for that matter.

That day I told Adele in a questioning sort of way, "I want to get my own wheelchair."

She winced a little and said, "I don't know if you're ready to be up in a chair."

I pleaded even though I knew the futility, "I've been getting on the tilt table twice a day."

Her rebuttal was, "And you almost pass out at forty-five degrees!"

Not giving up the cause, I said, "They have those chairs that recline."

To that, Adele said, "Let me check with Freddie Contreras."

Dr. Contreras was so young, and Adele always called him Freddie Contreras. So the first morning that they walked into my room for rounds after I started talking, I said, "What's up, Freddie Contreras?"

My whole care team fell out laughing.

Dr. Contreras said, "So the news is true."

I looked at Adele and said, "Have you been gossiping again?"

After everyone stopped laughing, Dr. Contreras asked me, "Now that you can talk, is there anything you need?"

Without hesitation, I said, "Solid food."

I weighed two hundred and five pounds at the time of my accident, but now my six-foot-two frame was down to one hundred and twenty-nine. The feeding tube came out that morning, and I got to order a special meal for dinner. The next morning, the first thing everyone wanted to know was how my dinner was.

With all seriousness, I said, "Please put the tube back in."

After they stopped laughing, Dr. Contreras asked, "Seriously?"

I replied, "Actually, it was delicious."

Barbara just said, "What are we going to do when this kid is gone?"

One weekend, this social worker who I had never met before came walking into my room and reached up and turned my television off. I told her, "I was watching that."

She told me, "I want to talk to you."

Trying to give her a fair chance, I asked, "Who are you?"

Proudly she said, "My name is Mrs. Green, and I am a social worker."

My first thought was, *Oh no, someone else trying to stick me in a group home making coffee mugs for a living.*

Then she said, "I brought some brochures of some group homes for you to look at."

I knew it, and without hesitation, I told her, "I don't want to look at them."

Then she said, "Young man, you need to start making plans for your future."

I tried to be forceful as a man in a hospital bed could be when I said, "I have plans for my future."

Mrs. Green asked me, "What are your plans?"

Knowing I was wasting my breath, I said, "I plan on walking again and going to college."

This lady who did not know anything about the real me said, "You are only hurting yourself by not making realistic plans."

Astonished at her insensitivity, I asked, "Why are you being like this?"

Mrs. Green told me, "I'm not the one being unreasonable."

I could not believe she was talking to me this way, and I demanded, "Please get out of here."

To that she replied, "I am not leaving until you look at these brochures and start making realistic plans."

I don't know how much she had heard, but Barbara stormed into my room and said, "Here are some plans for your future, sister. Get out of here."

Then she told her, "Do not come back in this room without me or Dr. Contreras."

My friend Less was a staff psychologist at John Sealy and had taken a special interest in me. Many times after his shift was over, he would come by my room and visit with me. Our talks would often turn to my feelings and frustrations although now I realize that he steered the conversation that way. Often he would sit there drying my tears with one hand and his with the other.

He came by that afternoon because he had heard all about Mrs. Green's attempt at making me a better man with a group-home spirit and an eye for coffee mugs. I was lying in bed staring at this big, yellow window shade hanging on my hospital room wall. After the accident, my friends had hung it on the wall in the hall of the high school, and then everyone had signed it for me. I spent many lonely hours reading the sentiments that my friends had written.

Less sat there beside me for some time before he said, "Some people will never see the heart that is inside of you."

As if he were very carefully considering his words, he paused before continuing, "They will not consider the odds that you have already overcome."

As he loved to do, he placed his hand on top of my head and said, "Don't let little people make you mad."

Finally I looked up at him and gave him one blink for *yes*. He smiled and said, "I am so proud to know you."

Not being able to just let it go, I asked, "What was her problem?"

Leslie said, "You can bet I will find out."

Then he grew very serious and told me, "Do not worry about people like her, and do not let them plant doubts in your mind."

As fortune would have it, I was going to go to a world-famous rehabilitation hospital in the Texas Medical Center for my rehabilitation. There were literally people who had traveled there from all over the world to rehabilitate from injuries or health problems. The Texas Institute for Rehabilitation and Research, commonly known as TIRR was such a miracle for me. A small-town farm boy who had picked more bushels of peas and beans than some countries consume getting the break of a lifetime. I had no insurance but did have a hospital staff at John Sealy who loved me and pursued a bed for me there with dogged determination.

One morning, my care team walked into my room for rounds, but the usual smiling faces were not there. The mood was very solemn, but this one respiratory therapist named Mandy was smiling from ear to ear. At least I knew they were not about to tell me I was dying. I tried to lighten the mood, asking, "Do we need some coffee?"

Dr. Contreras asked me, "While you are waiting on your bed at TIRR, how would you like to go home?"

I looked at Dr. Contreras and the rest of my care team to see a mixture of halfhearted smiles and teary eyes. My own eyes welling with tears and like a little child with a broken voice, I said, "I am not walking yet."

Suddenly tears burst from Adele's eyes, and she had to step out into the hall, and Barbara followed her to console her. Dr. Contreras lowered his head to look at some object on the floor as he took off his glasses and rubbed his eyes. After a short time with my words piercing through their hearts like a murderer's dagger, he said, "We know you will not give up."

Then he took his eyes of whatever he had been watching and said, "You have been here nine months."

In a couple of days, Mom drove down with one of her friends to bring me home. Most of the way home, I lay down stretched out in the backseat, but before we got home, I was in so much pain I wished I had never left the hospital. Mom would stop every few miles and try and help me reposition to ease my pain. The adventure was only just beginning.

When Mom pulled down our driveway, my dogs started barking like crazy; some way they knew that I was in the car.

My dad had rented a hospital bed for me and carried me from the car inside. Before he even got me in the bed, the phone was ringing; friends were calling for me. Darrell Howerton had called the hospital to talk to me, and they had told him I went home. That night I and my friends sat around my bed talking until after two in the morning. Then it was clear to me why they wanted me to go home and the effect it would have on my morale.

THE LEGEND

The next morning, I was lying in my bed watching television and smelling bacon fry for the first time in a long time when I heard a knocking at the door. I could see my dad walk past my door on his way to see who it was. When my dad opened the door and saw who it was, he said, "Hey, Steve!"

Steve Tackas said, "Hey, Big Jim, I heard Scooter was home?"

Dad said, "Yes, and where do you think that little slacker is?"

As Steve headed to my room, he said, "Some things never change."

When Steve walked into my room, he said, "It's almost eight o'clock, get out of that bed." Then he said, "Before I went to school, I had to come by and see you."

He walked over to my bed and pulled out a half-smoked joint and lit it. He stuck it in my mouth and said, "Get you a few hits of that."

I tried to protest, but he said, "Ms. Betty is cooking, they won't smell it."

With Steve holding the joint, I took three hits and stayed high all morning. Mom had been in the kitchen frying bacon, and Dad was sitting there smoking a cigarette and drinking coffee. Steve had always been able to talk me into anything with this one thing he would do. Steve would smile at you like he was Cool Hand Luke and make you think that you were his best friend in the world.

After a bi-district football game on my senior year, the entire team went to the Hot Biscuit in Longview for chicken fried steaks. As we were getting off the bus, Steve walks up to me, smiles big, and said, "Eat fast, I have got some killer."

I said, "After the way we just got our butts kicked, I need to get high."

We wolfed down our food and rushed outside to fire up. Steve looked at me and said, "We have got to get out of this wind so I can roll."

The only place to go was behind a shopping center about a hundred yards behind the restaurant. Even when we were between the building and a dumpster, the wind made it almost impossible to twist a joint. It was definitely every bit as good as Steve had claimed though, and we sat with our backs against the dumpster enjoying the high-grade marijuana. We got so stoned we could barely hold our eyes open and totally lost track of time. When we stepped out from behind the building, the buses had left the parking lot. I just stood there in dazed and confused, thinking about the fifty-mile, ensuing walk to get home.

The buses were about to turn off of the loop and drive past the building where we were. Without the hesitation that held me back, Steve ran out into the middle of the street and flagged down the first bus. A roar went up as we climbed onto the bus, but Coach Clark was not so happy. He stood up from the driver's seat and pulled me close and took a big whiff. The following Monday afternoon, we had to run one thousand yards of the dreaded belly drills. By the time we finished, it was getting dark, and there were over one hundred people watching. We ran from goal line to goal and had to drop to our belly and get back up and run each time one of the coaches blew their whistle.

We had drawn Dangerfield in bi-district because we were the second place team behind Pittsburg. They only beat us for the district championship because five starters, including myself, were expelled from school and could not play. We got expelled because of probably the most infamous plan ever conceived at our little high school.

The week before our game with Pittsburg was our bye week. Going into that week, we were tied with Pittsburg for first place, and when we beat them, we would be the first team in Winnsboro to win district in over ten years. As a team captain, I thought that we should have a party to celebrate. Monday afternoon after practice, we were in the parking lot behind the field house talking when I said, "Let's have a big party this week to celebrate."

Proudly Ronnie Yates said, "We party every week."

Rolling his eyes, Harold Wetzel said, "Scooter, you party every night."

Then I told them, "I mean a party that we can invite the whole town to." Going on, I said, "I'll organize people to bring all the side dishes and drinks and deserts."

Ricky Lopez looked at Carl Nelson and said, "I am afraid ask what the main course is."

Carl asked me, "Just what are you cooking up, Scooter?"

With a devilish grin, I said, "The biggest steak cookout in the history of Winnsboro."

Sheepishly Carl said, "I am afraid to ask where we are getting these steaks at."

To which I replied, "The steaks are everywhere."

That night under the cover of darkness, we went on our black-ops mission. We drove about fifteen miles outside of the unsuspecting city of Winnsboro down a lonely blacktop road. We took a gap down in a barbed wire fence and pulled Carl's truck out into the field. I walked up to a prize-winning Black Angus bull and put the barrel of my gun between his eyes and dropped him like a sack of potatoes. As soon as I fired that fateful shot, the six of us out there in that pasture fell out laughing. We laughed for so hard and for so long we liked to have never got that bull into the back of Carl's truck.

Ronnie and Harold worked in the meat department at Brookshire's, and after we skinned it, they took it there to process it. That Thursday night, we had our highly publicized party at the high school homemaking cottage. People from all over town were in attendance to support the team and enjoy the fellowship of other fans. There were tables spread out with cakes, pies, potato salad, baked beans, sweet tea, deviled eggs, and just about any other food you could think of. This rancher that I sometimes worked for had loaned us a big grill mounted on a trailer to cook the steaks on.

Our beloved principal, Mr. Carl Talbert, had retired after my junior year, and the man who had taken his place was dead set on going down in history as being the man who turned the hooligans at Winnsboro high school around. Mr. Talbert later told me that I was the reason he retired. He said he did not want to be principal my senior year.

The man who took his place looked for trouble in every move that I made and rightly so. Being young and dumb, we went into this plan fully thinking that he would just accept that fact that a group of teenage boys had come up with a truckload of steaks and were going to feed a small town. We had taken this kid with us who was not a senior, and our principal got to him, and he snitched us out.

The first steak was just hitting the grill when the police cars pulled up. Ronnie and Harold went into hysterics, and I turned to them and said, "Calm down, and let me do all the talking."

When Sergeant Peek got out of his car, I said, "You are just in time to have a steak with us."

To which he replied, "You boys are under arrest." Then he said, "We know where you got those steaks at."

This really ruined my plans to be a marine and make the world safe for democracy. On a weekend bus trip with other recruits, we had physicals and taken tests to qualify for our specialties. We were charged with felony theft for the bull, and it would end my career in the military and nearly my life. After this run-in with the law, and it was one of many, my future was crushed.

We were suspended from school for one week the day after our big cookout and did not get to play in the district championship game with Pittsburg. The guys still hung in the game, and we all felt terrible about letting our teammates and our coaches down.

Because we finished second place in district, we drew just about the toughest team in the country for bi-district. Among Dangerfield's many stars, they featured a future NFL Pro Bowl safety named Thomas Everett.

Toward the end of game, Dangerfield was ahead by forty-eight points, and a play did not get sent in from the sidelines. Our quarterback was a sophomore, and Coach Holt had told him in the event that a play did not come in to ask me what to call. I told him to run a sixty-series pass and look for Brent on the streak, but if he were not open to throw the ball to Thomas Everett. It was in the last two minutes, and I had not had a chance to hit the superstar up until now.

Brent was covered close, and Tim took me at heart and threw the ball straight to the all-state safety. Thomas had drifted back into a prevent defense and was thirty yards from any receiver. After he intercepted the pass that was actually thrown to him, he headed for the sideline with his eye on the end zone. I had an angle on him, but when I got to him, he put this little stutter step on me and froze me. As he ran past me, he tapped me on the face mask with the football. I am of Scandinavian descent, and I was screaming like a Viking as I ran along after him.

I was still screaming when I chased him across the goal line and screaming just as loud as I chased him across the end zone. Pine Tree Stadium in Longview has a chain-link fence around it, and I did not stop chasing the superstar until I had bounced him off that fence. Both benches and half of the stands cleared, and it took the officials twenty minutes to clear the field so we could finish the game.

After football, my drinking went from a weekend thing to every day and even on the way to school. Until that time, marijuana was the only drug that I or my friends used. After the cow incident, it went to anything that worked its way into my hands. At just eighteen years of age, it seemed as though any hope of a successful future was gone, and there was nothing to live for.

BACK TO WORK

The two weeks waiting for my bed at TIRR flew by, and before I knew it, we were driving back to Houston. I felt like a warrior going to battle as we drove down those beautiful East Texas highways to the medical center. For once in my life, I did not have anything to be cocky about, and the uncertainty of a demonstrable disability filled my mind. Telling people that you are going to walk again is easier than actually believing it when you are paralyzed. I could not even dress myself or get myself into a sitting position. I knew that there was a long way to go before walking anywhere.

When we got parked at TIRR, Mom went inside and got someone to help her to get me into a wheelchair. This one-story building did not look like much to me, and it was next door to a massive parking garage. There would be no such thing as an afternoon sun with this massive structure to the west of that one-story hospital. They must have put more concrete in that parking garage than there was in the whole city of Winnsboro.

A lady met us at the door from Administration to get all the paperwork filled out in admitting me to the hospital. Barbara asked, "Before we get you settled in and admitted, can I show you around?"

In an almost-pleading tone, I said, "I am hurting so bad from the ride down." Then continuing, I asked, "Can I just get in bed?"

Barbara said, "Absolutely."

Then she moved over behind my chair and proceeded walking at a brisk pace to my bed. After you went through the front door, there was a small waiting room with cheap plastic couches and a coffee table. There were a few people sitting there, reading and talking. Then there was a hallway straight ahead of the doorway that led to another hallway one hundred or so feet down. I could see people hurriedly passing by the intersection like so many couriers delivering important messages. Occasionally, you would see a wheelchair pass by so fast it was just a blur. I could only propel myself in a chair by kicking out with my left foot and going backward. Then it would only move a few inches at a time, and with each kick, it veered me to the right, and I had to use my left hand to get back on course. The old metal clunker wheelchair that I was in would have fallen apart if it had gone as fast as those people were going. Barbara was walking along, leading a lamb to slaughter in an antique wheelchair.

When we got to the intersection, Barbara pointed to a door across the hall to her left and said, "That is where your physical therapy will be." Pointing to her left and down the hall, she said, "Occupational therapy is that way."

Then she turned right and walked swiftly toward my room. As she walked, she explained, "Jimmy, we don't have any private rooms here."

My disappointment was easily noticeable when I answered, "My physical therapist told me I'd be in a ward with other people."

She explained, "Each ward has seven beds." Going on, she said, "We do have one semiprivate room with three beds."

That sounded good to me so I said, "Put me in that one."

Barbara told me, "That room is reserved for our most independent patients."

When she turned into my ward, which was the last one on the left, the gloom hit me hard. Each bed had these beige curtains that went around it for privacy, and all the curtains in the room were pulled. My bed was the second one on the right, and she placed the chair beside it and let the rail down. With the help of another nurse, they transferred me from my chair into bed, and the pressure was finally off my butt, and my mind was able to relax.

After Barbara got the paperwork in admitting me filled out, Mom got on her way home once again, leaving me; I was left to carry on alone. All of those feeling-packed conversations with my friends seemed like they were so long ago. My therapy would not get started until the next morning, so there was time to lay there in bed and get even more anxious about the work to come.

Before Barbara had left, she pulled a television down, which was on a retractable arm, and turned it on. The screen on the television was not very large, but when the TV was right in front of your face, it did not really matter. Using my left hand, I could actually change the channel by myself with concerted effort. Finding something that I could do by myself was encouraging, and I was flipping through channels without even noticing what was on them. Soon all the other curtains were open, but all of the beds were empty. There was a long, beige curtain that lined the far wall. It was still not clear what was on the other side of the hospital, but I was sure it was as dismal as the parking garage in the front. Just then a nurse walked into the room and went to that back wall and began to draw the curtains. As the curtains opened, I could not believe my eyes when I saw what those curtains were hiding. There were patio doors that opened up into Herman Park.

The next morning, all of my roommates were in their chairs and out of the room by eight thirty. I was lying there watching *Mister Ed* when Belinda Carlisle walked into the room pushing a wheelchair. I was actually thinking the lead singer for the Go-Go's came into the room and walked right up to my bed. The lady pushing the wheelchair introduced herself, "Hello, Jimmy."

She said, "My name is Donna Woodworth, and I will be your physical therapist."

Immediately I asked, "Do you know who you look like?"

She said, "Who?"

I said, "Belinda Carlisle."

Donna asked, "Who is that."

I said, "You know, the singer from the Go-Go's."

Then she said, "I don't look like her."

Assuring her I said, "Yes, you do."

Then in a genteel Southern accent, she said, "Me a rock star."

It had taken me awhile to catch on that she was jacking with me. She was such a dead ringer for the singer I am sure she heard the comparison all the time.

I asked, "Are we going to have trouble?"

Donna said, "Don't start none, and there won't be none."

She was going to be all right and had totally set me at ease.

She had brought the wheelchair to see how much effort it took to get me into it. I did not think there was any way she could get me into it by herself. This would not be the last time I underestimated Donna.

As she was letting the bed rail down, I said, "Do you have some help coming?"

Donna played it off, saying, "Who needs help?"

To which I replied, "You are not dropping me!"

Without stopping what she was doing, she pulled my legs off the bed. Next, she brought me up into a sitting position. She lowered the bed until my feet were touching the floor and locked her knees on mine. Without even a three count, she wrapped her arms around me. She snapped me into a standing position like she was doing a clean and jerk. When she turned me around and sat me down, I said, "Wow."

We were going to get along great because she was a joker to the bone. In this country accent, she said, "I been to the rodeo before."

One of the things that made me apprehensive about coming here was the fact that I'd be in a ward with six other men. I was so helpless that for some reason, I imagined conflicts coming up. I did not know that each bed had its own television, and I would not be at the mercy of stronger people. We lived in the country, before cable television came out that far. As the red-headed stepchild, it was my job to go outside and turn the antenna until the reception improved. I had learned to depend on certain cable television programs to break the monotony of the day.

The wheelchair that my occupational therapist brought me had quad pegs on the hand rims. Because of paralysis from the spinal cord, injury my hands could not grip the rims to propel the wheelchair. The pegs were designed so that paralyzed hands could push against them to advance the chair.

Even with the pegs, it was almost impossible for me to go anywhere. It was so hard to push, and this would get me so tired. If it were not for stopping every twenty feet to catch my breath, maybe going somewhere would not have taken as long. There were handrails on each side of the hallway for people needing support. By this time, my grip in my right hand was better. I found that if I turned around backward on the left side of the hall, I could use my left hand to pull on the rail. Still, we were a long way from warp speed.

On the first day of my therapy, I learned that I would see Donna and Savvy, my occupational therapist, twice a day. My afternoon physical therapy with Donna was right after lunch. After I was cleared to get up at my own discretion, I decided Donna should not have to walk all the way to the end of that long hall to get me. The first day that I decided to make it to afternoon physical therapy by myself, everyone in the hospital offered to help me by giving me a push. I was so intent to do everything myself and be a hero for my rock star physical therapist that I would not let anyone help me. There were people who passed me at least a dozen times and offered to help each time they passed.

At first, all of the physical therapy we did was on the mats at the back of the physical therapy gymnasium. Donna had to teach me to do stuff like rolling over by myself and getting into a sitting position. It was so frustrating because nothing we were doing seemed like it was going to help me get on my feet and walk again. The state was picking up the bill for my stay, and I only had ninety days to make as much progress as possible, and then they would put me out on my crippled butt. The rest of my life depended on the next three months at this great rehabilitation facility.

I made friends with a man on the other side of the room in the bed next to the patio doors. Walter Williams was from Toone, Tennessee, and had fallen while working on a power line and broken his back. His parents and his son, Donnie, were in Texas with him for his rehabilitation. Donnie was my age, and we hit it off immediately. Walter used to mess with me about his son liking me more than he did his own father.

There was still no movement in my right hand, and most of the things Savvy had for me to do in occupational therapy seemed pointless as well. Even then when no one seemed to give me any hope and when I was still in such bad shape, my vision for my recovery was way beyond any prognostication. I wanted to work on my strength and figured everything else would come naturally. I did not want to prepare for life in a wheelchair, because I did not plan to stay in one for the rest of my life.

I had to make every minute of my time there count, but I was still a teenager, and it was easy to have fun with all those great people. The hospital afforded me the opportunity to socialize with other patients and learn from them. Once we went to a trip to the Astrodome to watch the Houston Astros play. Our first baseline seats were in a leveled out area strictly for wheelchairs. At that time, I had no idea what a big deal this was. Nolan Ryan was Houston's starting pitcher; and from our seats on the second deck, we heard him let out an enormous grunt each time he threw the ball.

After the game, the field was transformed into a stage for a band that stands as American icon. The Beach Boys were so much fun, and I actually got to drink a cold beer with one of my occupational therapists. Sue Weller was so much fun. On the way to the astrodome, I was telling her about something that happened once when I was picking dry corn with Charles. Just for feed, Dad would plant acres of corn and let it dry on the stalk. He never would have approved of this, but I would pull the truck out in the field and throw the dry ears of corn into the bed and imagine I was a two-time Heisman Trophy winner at Texas A&M. When I gathered the corn up to the truck, I'd pull it up about one hundred feet and gather up to it again.

From her seat next to me, Sue leans over and says, "Hey, dirt farmer."

Then in this farm girl accent, she asked, "Can I buy you a beer?"

I had not had fun like this since before the accident, but I was so tired by the time we got back to the hospital. My normal sitting time was no more than two hours before taking a rest. With the game and the concert along with the commute both ways, I was over six hours when we got back. I had definitely been doing the two-cheek shuffle. That was where you shift from one butt cheek to the other to relieve pressure on your behind.

The night that we got back after dinner, but I had eaten an overpriced ballpark hotdog, had a beer and two Cokes, and as many peanuts as Sue could shell for me. There was a snack cart filled with all kinds of goodies that volunteers brought around nine depending on who was pushing the cart. The young lady pushing the cart on this night was the best part of a great day. Donna Hawkins was an angel sent to TIRR to save me from the demon of being alone. Remember, I am a nineteen-year-old boy by this time, and Donna was stunning. I lay there in my bed with my eyes transfixed on her on her every move. She was watching me watch her and stopped what she was doing and walked over to me. She walked up to my bed and looked down and said, "You have the most beautiful eyes I have ever seen."

From that very moment, I was in totally in love with this beautiful woman. She stood there talking to me for ten minutes. Finally, Walter called out in this feeble voice, "Jimmy, throw me some Cheetos."

In no time at all, it seemed like it were time to evaluate me for discharge. One day, Donna had just helped me transfer on to the mats when she said, "After we stretch, I want to get you on the standing cage."

The standing cage was a rail box that you stood in with straps on your knees for support.

Donna started getting me in the cage every afternoon for a few minutes. The first day on the cage, I stood up only five minutes but in a week was up to fifteen. One day at lunch, I grabbed a piece of pizza off my tray and asked Sue to give me a push to the physical therapy gym. She dropped me off at the intersection in front of physical therapy gymnasium on our way back down to occupational therapy. I sat there in the intersection eating my piece of pizza thinking about that standing cage. The only part where I really needed any help getting to my feet was the first little push when you first get your weight over your feet.

With my pizza finished, I headed into the gym to try and stand up by myself. The gymnasium was always empty during the noon hour, and I knew I'd be free to try to stand or fall on my own. After my chair was in position, I took my right hand with my left hand and placed it on the hand rail. I used my left hand to wrap the fingers of my right hand around the bar as tightly as I could. As soon as I let go, my fingers unraveled like wet plastic wrap on a softball. Loosely holding the hand rail, I put my shoulders forward and went for it.

I hardly went anywhere before the concession flag was thrown, and I flopped back down into my chair. *Now I am ready*, I told myself as I shifted into grunt force and pushed with everything there was to give. I was almost there but once again went back down. I knew that people would be showing up any minute, and my standing-cage adventure would be over.

I bowed my head and said, "God, I have taken it." Going on, I remarked, "I have never felt sorry for myself. My bad choices put me in this situation." Looking up I cried, "Give me the strength to stand."

I got dangerously forward, this time almost falling; I was either going to stand up or fall face-first. I was able to catch my center of gravity and start pushing though. Then I got my weight out over my feet and started up like an Olympic weight lifter going for the world record. Fighting with everything I had, I was inching into a standing position. My knees were almost locked, but then my upper body began to lurch forward. I was caught, unable to go on and doomed to fall. Then I heard the only male physical therapist at TIRR scream, "You got it, Jimmy!"

Then I heard Donna's Wisconsin accent say, "You can do it, Jimmy."

I got my knees locked and began the fight to get my shoulders up. I stood there looking down at my feet so proud of what I had just done. I heard a yell of this cute intern, and then everyone started clapping. I looked up and saw Donna right in front of me. After the clapping stopped, she said, "I am so proud of you."

Trying not to sound out of breath, I said, "Thanks."

Then she said, "You know you're not going anywhere?"

I pleaded, "What do you mean?"

Proudly Donna told me, "You are improving, and that means we can get you more time."

I looked up again and said, "You are so great."

Donna was able to get me ninety more days, so the wheels of improvement kept turning. I resolved within myself to work even harder for the next ninety days. That was the only way that I knew there would never be any doubt in my mind about whether or not I had done everything I could do to get better.

One of the things that really surprised the doctors and staff about me was how active I was. They had these odometers on the wheels of our wheelchairs to measure the distance our chairs traveled in the week between your care team meetings. My distance was always at least six times that of any other patient in the hospital. Once they told me that my distance traveled was more than everyone else in my room put together, the electric chairs included.

Unless it was after lights out, there was not too much of a chance of keeping me in my bed. There was so much to do here, and there were so many other people to have fun with. The afternoon that my care team announced to me that they had approved me for another ninety days, I sat out in that hallway intersection by physical therapy thinking back on the last fourteen months. Even though there was every reason in the world for me to be proud of my efforts, at times it was hard to be proud. A spinal cord injury is a strange bird, and no two injuries are exactly the same because of the amount of damage done to the spinal cord. I mentioned it earlier, but the spinal cord is involved in everything that takes place in our lives. If you do damage to your spinal cord and live, you are not faced with an easy road.

LIFE GOES ON

Sitting there in the intersection facing the front doors, I was feeling empty in a way. It had been so long since I was able to live the way that I always had. Life took me from always being in control to a place where I always needed help of other people. I needed someone my age to hang out with so desperately. Donnie was going to college and had a girlfriend, so I never got to see him anymore.

My head hung down in true-pity party fashion when I heard her calling out. I lifted my head and saw her outside of the glass doors, standing there in undefined splendor. Then two other girls just as lovely appeared. They were walking next to a guy wearing an AC/DC T-shirt, sitting in a wheelchair, wearing mirror shades. Another guy who looked to be my age was pushing his wheelchair for him. Two of the girls opened the double doors, and the other girl came in to open the inside door. This guy was surely a character, and it looked as though I was going to be receiving the benefit of his company. I watched them all the way down the hall. They turned right to go toward my ward, and this guy looked at me and said, "Peace, brother."

I guess for the effect, he shot me a peace sign.

Not to be undone, I gave him a thumbs-up and replied, "Be groovy, pimp."

They laughed so hard everyone down the hall turned to look at us to see what was so funny. They pushed Huggy Bear to the same room that I was in, and just like that, another need filled. There were two empty beds in my ward, and by afternoon, the other bed had been filled with an eighteen-year-old surfer. Before long, Steve and Greg, rocker and surfer respectively, were like my shadows. They were both from Houston, and there was a steady flow of kids my age in and out of our ward.

One Sunday evening, Steve came into our room and rolled up to my bed with this stupid grin on his face. He had been out all day with some of his friends, and he looked like Cheech and Chong put together. I cracked up laughing when I saw him and asked, "How many bong hits have you had today?"

Steve looked around and then lamented, "Several."

Then he looked around again like he was James Bond and asked, "What are you doing?"

Firmly I replied, "You big dummy, what does it look like I am doing?"

Steve looked at me with a Harpo smile and said, "Get up, Mr. Independent." Then he added with a wink "I have a treat for you."

By this time, I could get into my wheelchair by myself and kept it within reach of my bed. I got into my chair, and Steve went across the room to get Greg out of his bed. Greg had been in bed long enough that he could get back up, but he had to wait for nurses to transfer him into his chair. Steve and I were out on the patio when he held up his hand and said, "Look what we got."

In his hand was a marijuana joint that looked like a quarter pounder. Immediately I looked toward the door, then back at him, and asked, "Are you stupid?"

Like an idiot, he said, "What?"

Explaining in a childlike tone, I said, "We can't smoke dope out here, you goober,"

Steve said, "Relax, we are going out in the park."

The patio doors opened, and a nurse helped Greg outside. Wanting to fit in, I agreed, and we started a quadriplegic convoy out into Herman Park. If you are in a hurry to get anywhere, the last thing you want is to be behind three quadriplegics if they are in manual wheelchairs. After going about fifty yards out, we got off the sidewalk another twenty yards. Moving my chair in the grass was the hardest I had worked since coming to TIRR. After we are off the sidewalk about fifty feet, Steve put the joint in his mouth and held the lighter up to it. That's when we made the discovery that none of us had the dexterity to light a cigarette lighter.

It was a really hot summer day, and Greg looked at Steve and said, "Hold it to the metal on your wheelchair."

Rolling his eyes at him, Steve said, "You dork, let me just use my heat vision."

I noticed this guy walking across from us and held up my hand to get his attention. Steve said, "Don't call him over here!"

Greg said, "Let's get out of here!"

Agreeing I said, "Y'all run."

When the guy got to us, I handed him the joint and the lighter and said, "Light this for us."

Without saying a word, he lit the joint and put it in my mouth, pocketed the lighter, and walked off.

I took a good hit and while holding it in said, "We better not let this go out."

Steve asked emphatically, "Did you let him take my lighter?"

Looking at him with a grin, I replied, "I did not let him. He just took it."

It felt so good to really be able to relax and enjoy the park on that wonderful day. That time Steve Tackas had sparked up in my bedroom, I had caught a buzz, but it was not like this. Until that night I had never moved the fingers on my right hand. After that, whenever you saw me, I was flexing them. I had reservations about smoking and gave in only because I was worried about what Steve and Greg would think. The nurses from our station stood at the patio doors watching us the whole time, ready to spring to action if we needed their help. They referred to us as the delta nine transportation society after that.

I was making minimal progress, but it was coming so slow it could hardly be noticed. Even from the mats in the physical therapy gymnasium, which were lower than my chair, I could transfer into my wheelchair on my own. I could pull up to the standing cage and easily get myself into a standing position. The nurses no longer had to change my bed every time I fed myself. I could dress myself now and even get my socks on.

Even with my new friends, after all of those months in the hospital, depression was setting in. One Saturday morning, I was on the patio sipping a cup of coffee. I loved to be on the patio and enjoy Herman Park in the morning. When I was alone with my thoughts was the only time I did not have a disability. In my mind I could be anything that I wanted to be and go anywhere my imagination would take me. On this morning, my imagination was out of gas, and the only place there was to go was deeper and deeper into depression.

The patio doors slid open, and a nurse said, "Jimmy, you have a phone call."

I turned and asked, "Who is it?"

Ann said, "I am not your secretary." She finished by saying, "You better get in here and take this call."

It did not matter who it was; this was a reason to get excited. I turned my chair, and Ann moved to help me get over the tracks of the patio door. There was a bedside table next to my bed with a phone, which had the receiver lying next to it.

I picked up the receiver and said, "Hello."

A very cheerful voice from the other end said, "Hey, Scoot, what's up."

There was no doubt as I said, "Jan Wilkinson."

She was a lifelong friend and was just the right medicine for me at this moment. She asked me, "Buddy, how are you?"

I thought about what I was going to say for once in my life and asked, "Do you want the truth?"

Jan asked, "Do we need a pep rally?"

Jan was head cheerleader when I was junior, which was her senior year. She was elected football sweetheart, and being the player that nominated her, she asked me to be her escort. When she received the award at halftime was the first and only time that I kissed my friend. There had been a picture of this tiny cheerleader standing next to me on the front page of the newspaper. All of the other escorts got to take their helmets off and go into the field house and comb their hair before the ceremony. I was the deep snapper and was on the field with the kicker's right up until the ceremony. Then my hair was so thick, curly, and sweaty that when I took my helmet off, it looked like a wet dog.

Then she asked me, "What is the address where you are?"

Thinking she wanted my mailing address, I said, "If you send me a cake, put a file in it. I am ready to get out of here."

Jan told me, "I am in town and want to come see you."

After I got off the phone as hurriedly as a quadriplegic could hurry, I put on a clean shirt and washed my face and brushed my teeth. Then I went back out on the patio and tried to look cool while I waited for my friend. Early every Friday afternoon, Greg and Steve left the hospital on weekend passes and were not back until late Sunday night. Weekends were the hardest on me, and getting through them was like sleeping through an extended-length nightmare. I spotted Jan as she walked in to the room and watched a nurse point to the patio. She walked toward the patio doors with her eyes on me, and I remembered so many things that we had done together. When she slid the patio door open, she chimed, "My Scoot."

In reply, I said, "You are a sight for sore eyes."

Since I had been at home, I had gained about fifteen pounds. The first thing Jan said was, "You are a little fatty." Then she put her arms around me and said, "You look great!"

She gave me a big hug, and I asked her, "Can we go out into the park and talk?"

Jan told me, "Of course, we can."

I pointed to the nearest picnic table and said, "Let's go over there so you can sit down."

We sat out in the park talking about nothing in particular for a couple of hours. We talked about things that were troubling me, and we both sat there crying. For a while, Jan just got up and stood there and held me and did not say anything. Just like when I was in high school, nearly everything I did centered on what I thought people would think of me. After all that time of being in the hospital and not walking yet, people were surely thinking that I had given up on myself. She let me know that no one thought that, and I had a whole town pulling for me and proud of me. Before my friend left, she took me back inside so that I could get into bed. As I watched Jan walk out of the room, I wondered if she had an idea how much she had just blessed me.

The days rolled by, and the progress was so slow it could hardly be noticed at all. It was clear to see that even with the additional three months, I was not going to go home walking. Savvy had got me measured and all set to receive my very own personalized wheelchair. My first choice in color for my wheelchair was hot pink, but because of availability with the pegs, we went with red and black. It would not be there by the time my discharge came, but it was in the works. If there is one thing you learn after sustaining a spinal cord injury, it is to be patient.

One day in physical therapy toward the end of my stay there, I was on the mats with Donna. There was this guy who was my good friend who had one arm and a leg blown off in an electrocution.

The skin and the scars were testimony of the excruciating pain that this young man had been forced to endure. From the mats at the back of the gym, Donna and I watched my friend climb the staircase to the second floor loft of the gymnasium. When he got to the top, everyone in the gym gave him a round of applause. When my physical therapist looked down at me, it was the first time she had ever seen me cry. Her response was perfect and lifted me from a pit of self-pity. She leaned down, and as she embraced me, she said, "One day you will do more than that."

Rubbing my eyes, I asked her, "Do you really think so?"

Without hesitation, she told me, "The way you work, absolutely!" Then she added, "When I first evaluated you it was a different story."

After six months at TIRR, I went home in the same antique wheelchair that I arrived there in.

This time things were a lot different at home than when I came home from John Sealy Hospital to wait on my bed at TIRR. I could get myself in and out of bed and even stand up out of my chair and get into the bathroom. I was not going to be walking the railroad tracks with Charles and Robert, but then I was not going to be stuck in bed all day either. On my first morning home, we had to get up early and go to a meeting at school. I still had a semester of school to finish before graduating from high school.

That day when we got to the school, I created a big disturbance in the halls. Everywhere we went kids were pushing each other out of the way to get to me, and some were even leaving their classrooms to talk to me. Jan had tried to tell me that going through the trials that I had fought my way through had made me a hero to people. I was going to go to school for half a day and spend one period of that in a special education class to get any help that I might need.

Albert and Robert would be there every morning to get my wheelchair out of the trunk and get me in the building. That was a big help to Mom because that old metal wheelchair was hard on her. After all those years of abuse at the hands of me and Charles, Robert was as tough as nails. He told the freshman boys, "If Scooter comes to a door and one of your not there to open it for him, and I will whip every one of you."

Albert Lopez had an older brother who was my age named Ricky. They moved to Winnsboro when I was in the eighth grade from the West Texas city of Lubbock. Their father was single and ended up raising half of my classmates at one time or another. It seemed like any time one of my friends ran away or had any kind of falling out with their parents, John Lopez took them in. The summer between my junior and senior year, my dad's authority became too much for me, and I lived with the Lopez's. I will always refer to that as the summer of adventure and for good reason.

We all lived in a one-bedroom apartment with an old, fold-out couch in the living room. When the couch was folded out, there was this metal support bars that crossed the bed in two sections. One of those bars crossed the folded-out bed approximately at the small of your back and the other just below the knees. The only way that we could be comfortable on this nightmare-causing bed was to sleep crossways. John was a truck driver and was on the road most of the time, so it was not always the three of us lying crossways on a fold-out couch.

Robert probably could have given all the freshman boys a beat down at the same time, with letting them draw first blood. We stopped picking on him by his seventh-grade year, and by the time he was a freshman, he had whipped us both. He would fight three or four people at once, and win. Robert and Charles's mother used to tell us one day we'd be sorry, and we just laughed it off.

One of the classes that I had was Coach Milford's government class. The second day I got to this class, Coach was late, and I decided I'd show off and transfer into a desk. My friend Sharon Swann was in this class and was helping me transfer into the desk when we heard Coach Milford's voice, "Scooter, what are you doing?"

Looking over her shoulder toward the door, Sharon flippantly replied, "He is going to sit in a desk."

Advancing toward me, Coach answered back, "He is going to break his neck again."

A voice from the back of the room chimed in, "Relax, Coach, he can do it."

Coach replied, "I watched this boy grow up. Don't tell me relax."

By that time, I was in the desk and pleaded, "Relax, Coach."

The first day of class, Coach Milford tells me, "Scooter, put chair your by my desk."

I asked, "Why, Coach?"

Coach looks at me tenderly and said, "If you need anything, I'll help you."

So after he calls roll, Coach Milford looks at me and asked, "Do you need anything?"

I looked at Sharon and gave her a wink and said, "A beer and a hot dog."

After the class stopped laughing, Coach said, "A beer got you in that chair in the first place."

The same voice from the back said, "No, Coach, it was a bunch of beers."

One day in my junior year, we were in our defensive groups going over a stunt we were adding that week. We ran a five two defense, and I played the strong side-defensive end. Coach Milford was the defensive-end coach, and he was on a tear that day ranting about the importance of this particular stunt. As he walked along wildly gesturing with his hands and doing his best Bear Bryant imitation, I was walking along behind him mimicking his gestures. Coach Milford turned around and spotted me mocking him and, without considering the ramifications, slapped me as hard as he could.

My good friend Edward Williams laughed and said, "Don't kill him, Jimmy Drew!"

Sam Morris looked at me in disbelief and said, "I would."

Not believing what he had just done, Coach put his arms around me and said, "Scooter, I am so sorry."

Knowing that I deserved to be slapped, I told him, "Don't worry about it, Coach."

After practice, Coach Milford came out of the office and got me before I showered. When I stepped into the office, Coach Holt said, "Scooter, Coach Milford told me what happened."

Before he could say anything else, I told him, "Coach, I had it coming. Let's just let it go."

Coach Milford said, "Son, I slapped you."

Looking at him and smiling, I told him, "You did not slap me. My dad slaps me."

BACK ON MY FEET

In my special education class, Mrs. Arrington was using me to tutor the other people in the room. I had played football with Ricky Wells, and his little brother was in this class. We called his little brother Big Bird, for obvious reasons. One day I am standing up at this table relieving pressure, when James walks up beside me and takes my right arm and puts it over his shoulder. Then he looked me square in the eye and said, "Let's go for a walk."

Looking up at him, I exclaimed, "I can't walk!"

Pulling me closer to him, James just said, "Let's try.

Then compassionately, he added, "I will not let you fall."

Finally I agreed, and James looked at Keith Asberry and said, "Get up and get his other arm, fool!"

They walked me all over the classroom that day, and the whole class got involved by encouraging me. Mrs. Arrington saw how much trouble my right leg was giving me and said, "Scooter, try hiking your right hip and swinging your leg."

That helped a lot, and the encouragement of the class grew even louder, prompting the teacher from across the hall to come investigate.

Mr. Barnes exclaimed, "Why, Scooter, I did not know you could walk."

James said, "He didn't either."

Keith stuttered when he talked, but we got his meaning when he said, "Ca-ca-can't, can't keep a good man down."

Within a day, everyone at Winnsboro High School and a lot of people in town knew that I was walking, even though it was with help of my friends. My schoolmates were amazing because, after all that time in the hospital, they made me feel like a hero. They were proud of me because every prognosis that had been given me was very bleak. They were proud of me because in the face of insurmountable odds, I had not given up. By the simple act of me not giving up on myself, it left the door open for God to move in my life. After coming home from the hospital, the amount of exercise that I did every day actually increased. We had this upright piano in our dining room that worked much better than a standing cage. All throughout the day, I would pull my chair up to the piano and, after locking the wheels, and get myself into a standing position. Steve Tackas came by one day and brought me a couple of light dumbbells to work with, and Jerry White and Albert Lopez may have actually thought they were physical therapists.

One afternoon, Ricky and Charles were at my house hanging out and just talking. Some other friends came by for a while, and as they were leaving, Missy said, "Scooter, I always knew you would make it."

After she was out of earshot, Charles turned to me and said, "Bullshit!"

I asked, "What do you mean?"

I had wanted to believe that my friends believe in me, so I questioned them further, "Do you think she gave up on me?"

Ricky took me by the shoulder and turned me to face him so I could see his eyes. Then he said, "Hoot, I love you."

He caught me off guard, but I replied, "I love you too."

Ricky pointed to himself and then to Charles and said, "We thought you were dead."

Going on, he said, "Everyone thought you were dead."

After a while, even though school was so much fun, I saw that this was all too much on my mother. The old metal wheelchair that I was using was quite heavy, and her back started giving her trouble. My counselor from Texas Rehabilitation Commission had been working with me on me going to college somewhere, so I figured I'd jump into that. I got a study guide and began to spend my days studying for my GED. My plan was to take the equivalency exam and then start college at the junior college in Kilgore.

My mom drove me down to the Kilgore College center in Longview in to take my test to get my general equivalency. I had always been very smart but because alcohol and drugs never had applied myself in school, or anything much for that matter. The girl at the testing center who ran the test through the grader said I had the highest score she had ever seen before. That night, to celebrate, Dad grilled steaks, and we talked about where I wanted to go to college.

Early one evening while sitting on the front porch with Dad, this truck pulling a trailer came over the hill of our driveway. This man got out of the truck and introduced himself to my father. He said, "Mr. Pierce, my name is James Spicer."

My dad shook his hand and said, "It is nice to meet you."

Mr. Spicer then told my dad, "Barbara Cox told me that Scooter needs some parallel bars."

Barbara was my mother's friend, and he continued by saying, "I had this spare material lying around, so I welded some for him."

And that was the way I came to have my very own set of parallel bars in our yard. Mr. Spicer had even brought concrete to set them in permanently. Dad was building houses out at Lake Cypress, and before he would leave for work, he would push me across the grass out to my bars. To get to them there was forty yards of rough country ground to cover. Highway 11 is nothing but cows and chicken houses, so ours was not a neighborhood with manicured lawns and lush Saint Augustine grass.

Throughout the day, Mom would check on me to see if I wanted to come in, but I never did. The bars were thirty feet long, and at first, I would go down halfway and turn around. We lived on the very top of a hill, but from where the bars were, people could see me from the highway. People would drive by and see me walking and honk their horns and wave at me. Many times our yard looked like the parking lot at Wal-Mart from all the people who had stopped to watch me walk.

One day Mom comes walking out to the bars with this big grin on her face. As she approached me, she said, "I have good news for you."

Always ready for good news, I asked, "What is it?"

She said, "A physical therapist from Sulphur Springs just called."

Excitedly I asked, "What did they say?"

Happily Mom told me, "I am taking you for an evaluation Monday."

We had been waiting on this call, and all I could say was, "Praise God."

Donna had called them to get them to see me on an outpatient basis for physical therapy. My new therapist's name was Sam Savier, and the first thing I said to him was, "I am walking now!"

To which he replied, "I know, your mom told me when I called."

Then trying to contain his smile, he said, "I talked to someone that you know."

Thinking he knew one of my classmates or their parents, I asked, "Who?"

Finally letting a big smile come through, he told me, "Donna Woodworth."

Like a small child who had just spotted Santa Claus, I asked, "Did you tell her I was walking?"

He replied, "Of course."

Trying to contain my excitement, I asked, "What did she say?"

With another smile, he replied, "It sure took him long enough."

My countenance falling, I asked, "Did she really?"

Sam said, "No, she just told me to tell you that."

Then he told me, "She wants to get you back down to Houston for gait training."

My walking did not really have a gait to it, but the thought of going back to Houston and working with all those great people again excited me. The first day I got on the parallel bars, I stood up on my own and walked for Sam; it amazed him. The classification paraplegic and quadriplegic has nothing to do with the amount of paralysis. It is determined by the level of the break. A break in the first eight vertebrae results in quadriplegia. My break was an incomplete break at the third cervical vertebra. Sam was amazed to see someone with a break as high as mine get up and walk. I never thought that seeing my friends at the rehabilitation hospital in Houston would ever happen again. Upon leaving there, Donna had not talked to me about the possibility of me coming back for more therapy.

Making friends had always been an easy thing for me to do, and after my injury, it seemed to be even effortless. After six months at that rehabilitation hospital in the medical center, they held going-away parties for me in the different departments. I got cards from people who had never worked with me and only knew me from passing me in the hallway or me stopping by their office to chat. Going back to TIRR was like coming home again, and I was in love with a rock star there.

About three weeks went by before there was a bed for me at TIRR, and twice a week Mom and I made the twenty-six-mile drive to Sulpher Springs for physical therapy with Sam. For the first time I made the ride down to Houston sitting up in the front seat. It was so exciting to finally be making as much progress as I was making. This time would be a lot different because I could totally take care of myself. When we arrived at the medical center, we parked by the front door so I could get out of the car and walk in. The first person who saw me was the physical therapist Ronnie, whose encouragement gave me the fight to stand up for the first time.

He repeated Keith Asberry's words when he said, "Can't keep a good man down."

All of the beds in the semi-private room were empty, so it was actually a private room. I had only been in it for about an hour when Rick moved in and invaded my privacy. Rick was a paraplegic from a diving accident. He had been in this room several times before and knew all the ins and outs of this hospital.

Not long after Rick got moved in, the third and final bed in our room was filled. Big Chris Bullard had been injured in a football game, and naturally we hit it off. The three of us had so much fun together talking. Chris's mother lived close by and was at the hospital a lot. She kept us well fed with cookies, brownies, and homemade candy.

Chris was a Christian, and we talked about and shared our faith as much as possible. I told him about what it like for me when I died, and all he could say was, "Wow." This faith thing was new for me, and even I knew how weak that I was in it. Chris had been telling me about this person they knew who was a prophet who was coming to see him. I was not even sure what a prophet was, but it sounded good to me.

One day his mom came walking in our room with this lady whom I had never seen with her before. Big Chris looked over at me and said, "That's her."

After she gave her son a hug, Mrs. Bullard said, "Hello, Jimmy."

Then she turned to the lady with her and said, "This is our friend Katherine. She came to pray for Chris."

I said, "Hello, Mrs. Bullard, and hello to you too, Ms. Katherine."

That lady started praying for Chris, and I closed my eyes in reverence, but suddenly she stopped her prayer and spoke my name. She looked up at me and walked around Chris and came over to me and took me by the hand. She closed her eyes and held my hand for a moment then said, "Jimmy, I have a word for you."

She opened her eyes and asked, "What do your friends call you?" And then added, "They don't call you Jimmy, do they?"

I told her, "They call me Scooter."

"Well, Scooter," she said, "this is what God is going to do with you."

Her prophecy for me began. She started, "One day you are going to look just like you did before you had your accident, and you are going to do things that many people only dream of." She went on, "God is going to use you to touch so many people." Finally, with marked disappointment she told me, "You will never be completely over this injury. There will always be something."

I only weighed one hundred and forty pounds and never saw me looking the same again or doing anything that other people dreamed about. My eyes were filled with tears, and it was impossible to speak for the lump in my throat. After she left, Chris was so excited for me he could hardly contain himself. As much as I wanted to believe her prophecy, then it was just too much for me to see.

My ninety-day stay turned into six months again because of a brace that I got for my right ankle. Every time I would pick up my right foot up, the toe of my foot would roll down into something called planter flexion. The brace was called an AFO, an acronym that stood for "ankle foot orifice." This time upon leaving TIRR, I was walking with forearm crutches.

Although my life was irreversibly changed, now I could see a future. All I ever wanted from those early days in Galveston was to be able to take care of myself. Now I could envision a time when I would be able to do that. My life did not have to be great, and I knew my days of overachieving were over.

My first class was at eight in the morning and was an English 101 with Dr. Holt. I walked into the class a few minutes before the bell to find nearly every seat taken. I sat at the front of the room right in front of this guy in a leather jacket, white T-shirt, jeans, and biker boots. If Eddie had not have had long hair, he could have been the Fonz. He told me he was in band and that his name was Eddie Berlin. That afternoon, Eddie thunders into my driveway on his Harley. I saw and heard him pull into the driveway and got up and met him at the door.

When I opened the front door, Eddie said, "Let's go to Longview."

Leaning out to look into the driveway, I asked him, "How am I going to get there?"

Without hesitation, he said, "On my Harley."

Looking at him in amazement that he actually thought I would get on a motorcycle, I asked, "Are you crazy?"

Explaining in a fatherly tone, I said, "In the first place, I can't get on your Harley. And in the second place, I wouldn't be able to hold on to you."

In summation, I told him, "If that's not enough, I wouldn't be able to hold my right foot up."

Eddie just said, "Follow me outside."

In the backyard of the big house next door, there was a wooden picnic table. Eddie pointed at it and said, "We'll get you on the table and roll you off onto the bike."

Seeing the possibilities of that part of his plan, I asked, "What about me holding on?"

He held up a piece of rope and said, "We wrap this around us."

Before I could ask my next question, he took off his belt, and he said, "We'll hold your foot up with this."

To all this, I replied, "You do have it all figured out."

Eddie popped the clutch on his bike and took off out of my driveway toward Highway 31 as if we were drag racing. I lived on a one-way street, and he was going the wrong direction. He turned left onto Highway 31 and crossed over to the other side of the campus and took a left on another one-way street. We were going the wrong way on this street too, but Eddie had jumped up on the sidewalk.

We went screaming by Davis Hall where all the Rangerettes lived. There were several of them outside as we buzzed Davis Hall, and I heard Connie Roth say, "That is Scooter on that motorcycle."

We were very quickly approaching a corner with traffic coming from both directions. I was thinking after all the work to get back on my feet again; my life was going to end when one of those cars ran over us. However, when we came to the corner, Eddie laid that big Harley over making the turn and never got off the sidewalk. I screamed for him to let me off all the way to Longview.

I told my Texas Rehabilitation Commission counselor that all the walking was giving me a hard time. I had to leave an hour early just to go eat breakfast before my first class. He got me an electric scooter that made everything much easier.

One day I was touring the campus of Kilgore College and decided to cross over the crosswalk over Highway 31 into unexplored territory. When I started down the other side, my scooter picked up speed and was freewheeling out of control. I slammed into a concrete trash can at the bottom of the crosswalk and, flipping me out of it, landed facedown on the sidewalk. There were several football players standing there, and they fell out laughing. One of them walked over and said, "Can I help you, partner?"

I was upset because they laughed at me, and I said, "Get your hands off me!"

They stood there and watched me struggle to upright my scooter and crawl back up into the seat. Once I was back in the seat, I looked at them and said, "See you later."

I pressed on the accelerator, but nothing happened. Slamming into a concrete trash can at warp speed apparently is not good for electric scooters. I looked at the one who had offered to help me and said, "I am going to need some help."

He smiled at his friends and then told me, "You burnt that bridge, partner."

A look came over my face like, *"Man, I did it again."* They all laughed, and my new friends pushed me back to my house. As they were pushing me back up the crosswalk, I looked at the guy who had tried to help me up and said, "My name is Scooter. What is yours?"

They laughed so hard the four of them had to just stop and hold on. I asked, "Now are you laughing at my name?"

A big, tall Neanderthal pointed at the football player who tried to help me and said, "His name is Cooter."

I exclaimed, "You got to be kidding?"

They laughed even harder before resuming pushing. When they got me home, I invited them in for a while so we could talk. Cooter played strong safety, Brent was a defensive end, Lance was a linebacker, and Vance played center. When we walked into the entrance of the duplex, there was a smell of marijuana lingering in the air coming from my neighbors. Cooter looked at me and said, "You are moving to the dorms."

I looked at him and said, "You don't tell me what to do."

He just said, "You're moving!"

I really liked living in the dorms. The men's dorm rooms at Kilgore College were a lot like living in Motel 6 in that each room had a door opening up into the parking lot. Each room had a bathroom area with double sinks, a separate area with a toilet and shower, two beds, two closets, and a double desk on the wall by the door. To everyone's amazement, I had the only private dorm room on campus.

I started working out with the football team in the weight room, and when they practiced in the afternoon, I'd go to the stadium and walk on the track. By the end of my first semester, I was easily the most recognizable person on campus. One of my closest friends was a cheerleader named Sandra McClure. She had a very dark complexion with jet-black, shoulder-length hair. Even with all those Rangerettes, she was one of the best-looking girls I had ever seen in my life. The best thing about Sandra was she was always hanging with me.

I met Sandra in Mrs. Speer's office. Latane Speer was my government teacher and one of my best friends at Kilgore Junior College. She was the cheerleader sponsor, and I was always running into Sandra in her office. I was so in love with Sandra, but I had lived in my imagination so long that I was afraid to voice my feelings and misinterpret hers. She was so beautiful, and there was nothing more than friendship that she could possibly see in me.

Vance and Cooter would soon become my best friends and constant companions. We called ourselves the three musketeers, but the other football players called us the three stooges. Everywhere I went I would walk holding on to one of their shoulders. Cooter lived in Longview, and we spent a lot of time at his house with his family and friends.

One Saturday morning, I walked out of my dorm to see Brent and Bo stringing their reels to go fishing. Cooter and Vance showed up with their rods and tackle boxes and soon just about everyone who hadn't gone home for the weekend was preparing for the fishing trip.

Cooter looked at me and said, "You ready to go fishing, partner?"

I said, "I don't have a rod and reel."

Vance told me, "I have an extra one you can use."

Brent started laughing and said, "Your little, crippled butt is about to go for a long walk."

Intrepidly I asked, "How far?"

Lance said, "It's a half mile with fences to cross."

With apparent disappointment in my voice, I remarked, "I can't do that."

Quickly Cooter answered, "You are going!"

Bo said, "I've got a lawn chair in my truck you can sit in when we get there."

This pond that I thought we were going to was north of Longview, down this winding oil-top road. We pulled off the oil top at a gate and the five other vehicles that was in the precession parked around us. I was riding with Vance and Cooter and asked, "Why don't we pull through the gate?"

Cooter looked at me like I was stupid and said, "We don't have a key, Einstein."

I didn't like what I was thinking they were going to do, so I asked, "How am I crossing that fence?"

Cooter bellowed, "Would you stop whining!"

Getting mad, I said, "I am not whining."

Trying to calm things down, Vance said, "Let's go figure it out."

The general consensus was to pass me through two strands of barbed wire—with the wires being held apart. Indignantly I told them, "That is not about to happen!"

Cooter asked, "Have you got a better idea?"

I said, "Hold the bottom wire up, and I'll roll under it."

Next I told them, "On the other side, someone picks me up."

On the other side, Brent got on his knees and said, "Scooter, get on my back."

Relieved I said, "Thanks, Brent."

He told me, "I just don't want to wait on you."

We had to cross a creek and another fence before we came to the largest pond I ever saw. It was at least a half mile to get there, and they took turns piggybacking me all the way to it. They set me up on the dam with a simple, white beetle spin lure that I picked out from among a truckload of lures, and then they scurried off like cockroaches with rod and reels.

I know the twenty or so football players who were out there wore a trail around that ten-acre lake. They were throwing crank bates, spoons, jigs, and every color of plastic worm you could imagine. Ultimately, they all ended up standing around me fishing from the dam. I sat in my chair on the dam and caught as many fish as they did put together. The longest cast I had all day was about thirty feet.

When we got back to the dorms, we were all outside in the parking lot talking. I had learned long ago to use my paralyzed hand to tie my shoes. When I reached out to do it a lot of the time, my wrist would spasm like a baseball card flapping in the spokes of a bicycle wheel. From the lawn chair that I had been fishing in, I leaned down to tie my shoe, and my hand started to spasm.

Michael Cooper said, "That's why you caught all those fish."

I looked up and asked, "Why?"

Coop said, "Because you have that natural jigging action."

When I say we fell out laughing, I mean it literally. There were three-hundred-pound linemen on their hands and knees laughing so they could not breathe.

NEW YEAR'S DAY

When the football season started, you could always find me standing on the sidelines with the team during the games. One Friday afternoon, the guys came to my room to get me for the pep rally. The pep rallies were all ways the same thing, and I was tired from a lot of walking that day. Apologetically I told them, "I am going to sit this one out, guys."

Cooter sneered, "No you are not."

Glaring at him, I said, "You do not own me."

Vance said, "He does today. Get up."

There was no use arguing with them, so I got up and walked down to the gym for the pep rally. I sat on the bottom row with the captains, and I was not a happy camper. I did not like the idea of being forced to do anything. Then Coach Miller got up to speak.

As the big man approached the microphone, we could hear him clearing his throat. He looked at the fifteen hundred people looking at him and said, "Every now and then you will meet some rare individual who will inspire you with their determination and courage."

Coach Miller looked at the players behind him and said, "We have been blessed this season with someone like that in our midst."

I turned and looked at James Latham, and he had tears in his eyes. James was as tough as Houston's Fifth Ward had every produced, and it made me wonder, *Is Coach Miller talking about me?*

I missed everything else he said, but when the applause started, I looked back at Coach Miller. He was holding up a jersey with the number 1 on it and my name on the back. Cooter got up from beside me and said, "Let's go, partner."

As I rose, the Rangerettes, the band, and everyone else in the gym went berserk. It was so loud that I could not hear what Cooter and Vance were saying, and they were right beside me.

When we got to Coach Miller, he calmed the crowd down and said as he put the jersey in my hand, "Scooter, you are a big part of this team."

At that very moment, Connie Roth yelled, "We love you, Scooter!"

I turned my head toward the Rangerettes, and Coach said, "Scooter, would you look this way for a moment?"

Everyone laughed at that, and then Coach said, "We want you to be our captain."

There was no way I could have made a speech. As loud as it were before, it was even louder now. The ovation was so long that it ended the pep rally. On the way out, Dean Webb stopped us and said, "Scooter, very few people will ever know the feeling of an ovation like the one you just received."

I looked at him and said, "It was cool."

He showed me the goose bumps on his arms and said, "It was past cool, son."

Cooter said, "I don't think any of us will forget this day."

The next night, we played at home, and I walked out to the center of the field with Cooter, Vance, Brent, Lance, and James to a much bigger ovation. I even got hugs from the captains on the other team. Since I was now officially a member of the team, I even got to eat in the training room, and that meant chowing down at every meal.

After football season was over, we played a lot of golf until time for intramural softball to begin. The football team was going to have two teams; the freshman and sophomores would each have their own squads. Since Cooter and Vance and all of my other good friends were sophomores, I was the manager of their team. We won the intramural tournament easily, ten-run ruling every team we played. It did not matter one bit who played because everyone on the team could leave the yard on any pitch.

Going home for Christmas break was actually a letdown. After all that time of living in my mind, life was so exciting. On the section of highway where my house was, we didn't even have cable television yet. A couple of days after Christmas, I talked Mom into taking me back to my dorm room. She did not want me to be alone on New Year's Day when we always had a big day at home with a table full of food and all-day football. At least there, I would have cable television to get me through the long, cold days.

During the holiday season that year, East Texas was the victim of Arctic-like ice storm that left ice on the ground for a month. There was actually a thick sheet of ice on the ground for over three weeks, and there was nothing for me other than the television. Being icebound in my dorm room was just a little bit better than being icebound at home. My electric scooter was like a sail boat in a hurricane when I got out on the ice, and venturing outside on it was useless. My cousin lived a couple of blocks south of the Rangerette Museum, and we planned to get together and watch the bowl games at his house on New Year's Day, but the only way I had to get there was to walk.

I looked outside on New Year's morning, and the parking lot looked like a polar ice cap. The very middle of the sidewalks was starting to clear from the sun, and I thought I could make it if I stuck to the sidewalk. I bundled up with everything I could get on before setting out on my mission. It was hard for me to hold on to my crutches if I was wearing gloves, so I left that morning for the three-block walk to George's house bare handed. I could not help but feel like Admiral Byrd trekking to the pole.

I was freezing cold before I had even made it out of the parking lot. With a spinal cord injury, everything that takes place in your body is impaired. Even your blood circulation is not as good, and without a good flow of blood, the body gets cold quick in severe temperature. As I arrived at the street, I was having second thoughts about this expedition. It was about a 150 foot walk to the corner, then a turn to the left, and another hundred and fifty yards to the Lee Street. From there I took another right and walked one block to my cousin's house.

Surveying the situation, I saw that by walking through the backyard of the house across the street and the cutting across the parking lot behind the Rangerette Museum would take almost fifty yards off my walk. It was a no-brainer, and so I stepped off of the curb into the slushy street. I could not get my boots on, so I was marching across the slushy ice in the street in my running shoes.

Walking through that yard was easy; in grass, ice crunches under your feet. Even though it was so cold it hurt my bones, it was great to be outside. When I looked up and saw that frozen parking lot behind the museum, it shot fear through me, and momentarily the cold did not register. Now it was either lose precious energy by backtracking or advance with caution across the ice on that frozen parking lot. Before setting foot on the ice, the thought of what I would do if I fell did not enter my mind.

I was moving ever so slowly on the ice, inching toward the other side of that parking lot. There were trees and shrubs all the way around the lot with the only exceptions on the driveway directly behind the museum. As I inched across a thick sheet of ice, my moves slowly became more fluid. As my confidence grew, the speed of my walking increased, a mistake that would eventually leave my entire face bleeding.

Suddenly my left crutch slipped out from under me, and I went down fast and hard, hitting the ice face-first. The pain that the ice inflicted on my face seemed to burn through my head even after I lost consciousness. When I opened my eyes, the blood that had poured from my brow was frozen and coagulated. Batting my eyelids like a genteel Southern belle to get them to open, I wondered how long I had been on the ice. Immediately the gravity of this situation hit me hard; I knew this was a life-and-death situation. The temperature was around twelve degrees, and I figured there were about ten hours to get off the ground.

There was a maintenance truck only thirty yards from where I was laid out on the ice like a harpooned seal. Even through the cobwebs hanging in my head, getting to that truck was a clear plan. Maybe it would be unlocked, and somehow I could manage to get inside. One at a time, I gathered my metal forearm crutches and threw them toward that truck. I would crawl on my hands and knees until I got to it and then get inside.

It was a struggle to roll onto my back so that I could sit up. In a sitting position, with my weak abdominal muscles, I was like a man standing on a ball. It was a struggle like never before presented to me to maintain my balance. My right side, the paralyzed side, made it close to impossible. The labor to sit up and the struggle not to fall were taking all of my energy, and I kept falling and would have to start the process over. Now my left brow was bleeding again, and my nose and lips were flowing with blood as well. There was no time to waste in trying that again, so I started to wiggle and squirm slowly, inching toward my crutches. It took me at least an hour to get to that maintenance truck, and I was very wet, and then it was time to get to that door handle.

The only way I was going to get up to that door handle to get into that truck would be to sit up again and then roll over onto my hands and knees. I was so cold that I felt the pain of frostbite creeping into my bones, and the stiffness of hypothermia was taking over my body. The only option that there was for me, other than lying there and dying, was to get onto my knees and open that door. It surprised me a little to get into a sitting position as easily as I did, and I could only hope that rolling onto my knees came that naturally. Sitting there thinking about how I was going to do this and wobbling like an egg standing on end, I twisted and fell to my weak side. After a couple of more falls, exhaustion took over, and all I could was lay there on my back and gasp for air.

Lying there on the ice, I rolled my head over and I saw an oasis; underneath the truck was a small, oblong dry spot. In a few minutes, I was under that truck—somewhat out of the freezing wind. My ears were painfully cold as my toboggan was lying on the ice a good thirty feet from the truck. The thought of going back for the toboggan was not a viable option.

There was no plan, but just to lay there and try and stay warm and pray that God would send me an angel. At the one spot in that backyard where there was a place to get through the shrubs, there was broken glass and limbs on the ground. I had almost fallen there, and there would be no way to squirm out of that break in the shrubbery. The time passed by so slowly, and I could almost feel my blood pressure dropping. There was a thick steam rising up from the ice as if to say the cold were deadly and that same steam would carry my soul upward in due time.

When the sun started to go down, I began to hear traffic on the street beside the museum. It was probably people out looking at Christmas decorations or cheerfully going to season festivities. I wondered what they would do if they knew a man lay dying a horribly painful death so close by them. How would my family and my many friends react when they learned the news of the way I died? That night, the temperature was going to get down to zero, and I was going to close my eyes, but never wake up.

From where that truck was to the driveway behind the museum was close to one hundred yards. I had to get to that drive and get out into the street if I wanted to live through the night. I began to squirm, and at the edge of the truck, I paused to say a prayer. I had been praying all day under that truck but knew this would be my last. I knew one way or another when I got out from under that truck that I was going to live or die.

In a calm but shaky voice, I said, "I've never given up. I have never felt sorry for myself." Now pleading, I said, "I pray and ask for help, but I don't beg." My last prayer of the day finished with, "I am begging for your help now."

When I opened my eyes and looked toward that driveway, my prayers were answered. Headlights of a vehicle turning into the parking lot were a sight for sore eyes. I watched them drive behind the museum, down past the gymnasium, and stop. It was another maintenance truck, and I quickly got over to the other side and got my good arm out and started waving and calling out.

The truck turned around and was slowly headed out of the parking lot. As I watched them drive past me, I cried, "God, don't let them leave me!"

The truck drove to the street, but even though no there were no cars coming from either direction, it stopped. It just sat there with its brake lights casting a red glow on the museum behind for about a minute. Then the brake lights went bright, and they backed up about one hundred feet and stopped for a few seconds. Then suddenly the driver dropped the truck in drive, and they raced up to me and stopped. Both doors on that truck flew open, and one of them yelled, "We are here, Scooter!"

When they got to me, they asked, "How long have you been here?"

I told them, "All day."

By the time they had me in the truck between them with the heat on high, they were both in tears. The man on the passenger side had his arms around me and was holding me close to him. They both wanted to take me to the hospital, but I promised them that if they got me to bed, everything would be fine. They stayed with me for a while and helped me get into dry clothes. They had been watching bowl games all day, and at half-time of the Rose Bowl, they just wanted to get out of the house. As they left my room, I knew God had sent them to save my life. I had been praying all day, but it was not until I decided to put some action behind those prayers I got my answer.

I started drawing a social security disability check and with the help of my dad had a plan to get a loan for a new truck. I saved up five hundred dollars and put it in a savings account at a bank on the other side of campus. I borrowed five hundred dollars against the money that I had in the bank. As soon as I paid it back, I would have credit at that bank. I was sick of going through the drive-through on my electric scooter.

I paid the loan off, and a banker at that bank approved for a loan to get a truck. My friend Paul Butler was going to be there with me that summer. I had wanted to meet him, and the first time I ever got close to Paul, I said, "My name is Scooter."

Paul gave me a look and said, "I know who you are."

Then I said, "How do you know me?"

He replied, "Everyone knows who you are."

So I said, "And you are the great Paul Butler, able to leap tall buildings in a single bound."

Nonchalantly he said, "Just white boys."

One day we were sitting in the training room eating lunch, and I told Paul, "My banker approved me for a loan to get a truck."

Paul took a bite of a fish stick, and gag reflex contorted him, and he covered his mouth with a napkin and quickly purged his mouth of the battered nastiness. He wadded up the napkin and, with a twenty-foot hook shot, threw it in the trash. Next, he looked at me and said, "Get your Rockefeller butt up and go get me a cheeseburger."

Seriously I asked, "Would you like fries with that?"

Standing up, he picked up my tray and his and said, "We're going to Juicy's to get a real cheeseburger."

Paul took me to Longview to Bass Chevrolet to look for my new truck. The first one the salesman showed me was a really nice, charcoal-gray with chrome wheels. The truck was about three thousand more than my banker told me that I could spend. Paul took the salesman off to the side and talked him into knocking three grand off the price. It was so easy that I called the bank and actually drove the truck home that day.

That summer, Paul and I did everything together. We went to the weight room every day and walked a lot. I would hold on to Paul's shoulder, and just like Cooter, he would try and walk off and leave me.

The next year, all of my buddies had transferred out to four-year schools to finish their eligibility, and the football players would not let me be their manager when it was time for softball. They told me I could be the assistant manager. They thought I taunted them too much when the sophomores were ten-run ruling them last year. I started my own team called the Scrubs, and we beat the football players.

Last year the football players had a sponsor paid for our game jerseys. This year, Gibson Drilling bought us entire uniforms. To mock us, the football team wore white T-shirts with names and numbers scrawled in Black Magic Markers.

GOLF COURSE MISSILE

My best friend after all the sophomore football players transferred out was a quarterback that transferred to Kilgore Junior College from the University of Texas. Cooter introduced me to his friend Mark Wright and asked Mark to look out for me while he was gone. Mark played on the Scrubs and hit two home runs in the game where we beat the football team.

Mark was crazy about Sandra and was always after me to fix him up with her. There was no way I was going to hook a beautiful girl that I was crazy about with a dog like Mark. He was my dog, and I loved him, but no Sandra. One day, Sandra and I were sitting in Latane's office talking. Latane knew very well how I felt about Sandra, and she thought it was funny how I protected her from Mark.

We were laughing when Mark walked through the door, and he asked, "What are y'all laughing at?"

Latane said, "I just mentioned your name, and they started laughing."

Mark sullied up and asked, "Really?"

Sandra told him, "Don't be so sensitive."

That made me laugh like crazy because I was always telling him that, only I put this girly emphasis on the word *sensitive*. To be funny, Sandra had overemphasized the word as well. Mark looked at me and nodded his head toward Sandra and winked. Not to let him down, I said, "Sandra, he wants to ask you a question."

Mark kicked my foot and said, "You dirty dog."

Sandra did not like him kicking me, even though she knew he was playing. As she was swatting his foot away, she said, "What do you want, Mark?"

Where he got the courage from, I'll never know, but he asked, "Sandra, will you go out with me?"

As if she were already prepared for this question, she replied, "I don't have time to date."

Then she said, "You see how fast I have to eat so I have time to study."

Mark said, "You have to enjoy life, and we can go to Longview and eat and see a movie."

Sandra put her hand on my knee and said, "If Scooter goes, I will."

Mark looked at me and said, "I hate you."

After my sophomore year, I was getting ready to transfer to East Texas State University to finish my degree in psychology. Vance was going to school there and could help me get acclimated. Cooter was home for summer break, and I was hanging out with him in Longview until the last moment.

We played golf every day that the weather permitted, and in this particularly hot and dry summer, that was every day. The way we made it competitive on the golf course whatever the par was on the hole was my par, only I started putting from the edge of the green at any spot Cooter picked. One day, Cooter had to take some papers from University of New Mexico, where he was finishing out his eligibility, to his mother at work to get signed.

Mrs. Kirkindoll was the head secretary at Marathon Letourneau, which was on the south side of Longview. After my sister was killed, we moved to Longview to be near my parents families. Then when my mom remarried to my stepfather, we lived on Fourteenth Street, which was just a few short blocks from where Mrs. Kirkindoll worked.

After he got his papers signed, we were on our way back up Moberly Avenue headed to Alpine Golf Course. Suddenly I pointed to a street and said, "Turn right here, and I'll show you where I used to live."

Cooter made a quick right and said, "You used to live in this neighborhood?"

Surprised that he actually made the turn, I replied, "Yes, sir."

He asked me, "Why didn't you ever tell me this?"

I told him, "It never came up."

I pointed to this old store across the street from a park and said, "Me and my best friend used to ride our bikes up here every day to get a Coke."

Cooter asked me, "What was your best friend's name?"

Not taking my eyes off the park, I said, "Michael."

He shot back with, "That's a good name."

Michael was Cooter's real name, but no one ever called him that, not even his mother. When we got to Fourteenth Street, I told Cooter to drive slowly because it had been a long time since I had even been on this street, much less lived here. Finally, I recognized my house and said, "I lived right there."

Cooter stopped his Blazer in the street and put it in park, and I sat there looking at our old house. When I looked back at Cooter, his eyes were welled up with tears, and I asked, "What's wrong, partner?

Cooter pointed to a house on Latham Lane and said, "I lived right there." Then he said, "I am Michael."

We sat there in the middle of the street for what seemed like an hour not saying anything. We each had big goose bumps on our arms, and we both had tears in our eyes. It was all coming back now, all the times we had spent together—his two older brothers and the forts we used to build on the creek behind my house.

I finally broke the silence by saying, "You know I used to whip you all the time."

Cooter said, "No, this was my neighborhood."

With a smirk, I replied, "Maybe when I moved away, it was."

Then I said, "And you ripped off my name when I was gone."

We parked and got out and walked down to the creek behind my old house. Sure enough, in the top of this old cottonwood tree directly behind my house, a tree house was still there, which we had built together. I asked Cooter, "Do you remember the day Neil McGruder fell out of the tree house?"

Cooter laughed as he said, "I think he hit every limb on the tree on the way down."

It had been eleven years since we had seen each other, and time had changed us both so much. Was this just a random thing that best friends would be separated as children then later become best friends again, and not remember each other from before? Eleven years and a broken neck later, destiny brought two best friends back together. Everyone was amazed when we would tell this story, and some did not believe it.

One Saturday morning, we were watching television at Cooter's house when his oldest brother walked in and said, "Let's go play golf."

Cooter looked at me and said, "Partner, you want to play golf?"

Without hesitation, I replied, "Let's go."

Everyone in Cooter's family went by a nickname. His father was Tomcat, his mother was Lightening, his middle brother was Worm, and Moose was the oldest. Moose told me, "Scoot, this has got to be a quick game. I have a wedding to go to today." Then he asked, "Will you just drive the cart today?"

I looked at him and said, "Duh, okay, Moose."

He hated it when we did that, and I think he started to have second thoughts about getting on the golf course with the two of us. He got the nickname Moose because he was so big, and it did not have anything to do with his intelligence. All the way to Alpine Golf Course, we were trying to get inside Moose's head.

Cooter looks at Moose and said, "Do you still have that problem shanking when you drive?"

Defiantly Moose said, "Don't start with me, Cooter. I can out drive you by thirty yards any day."

I had watched Cooter out drive a lot people and told Moose, "I don't see that happening."

Moose said, "What do you know about it? I taught Cooter to drive."

Grabbing the dash, I asked, "Who taught you to drive a car?"

Puzzled, Moose said, "What's that got to do with golf?"

Laughing boisterously, Cooter said, "You just ran a red light."

By the time we got to Alpine, Moose was mad enough to pull his own hair out of his head. Cooter went to get the cart, and I waited in Moose's truck. When Cooter got back, he smiled and said, "He is hot!"

I said, "We can't let up on him."

Cooter shot back with, "Not for a minute."

The first hole was a par three, and as Moose was lining up his shot, I said, "Give me a chew, Coot."

Cooter said, "I thought you had the chewing tobacco."

I asked, "You think we left it in the truck?"

Feeling of his pockets, Coot asked, "Did we even get it out of the television room?"

Feigning delirium, I said, "I need a chew bad."

Moose dropped his driver and walked over to his golf clubs and took a pack of Levi Garrett out of his bag. Then he turned and threw it hard right at my head. I ducked, and it barely missed hitting me.

I looked back up at Moose and said, "That was mean."

Moose just said, "I know how you two are. You work together like piss ants."

I said, "Just show us the long ball, Moose."

Coot laughed as he said, "He doesn't have a long ball."

As he was lining his drive up, I was truly afraid to say anything else. There was no need to say it anyway because he was furious. Moose drove the ball sixty yards over the green, and we watched it disappear into the trees.

With my hand shielding the sun from my eyes and searching for his ball, I asked Moose, "Was that the long ball?"

Using an imaginary pair of binoculars, Cooter said, "That was the too-long ball."

By the time we were on the seventeenth hole, Moose was ready to kill someone. This hole was a five-hundred-and-fifty-yard par five. Moose smashed the ball off the tee, and it soared right down the middle of the fairway like a rocket. At about two hundred and fifty yards, it started slicing. When Moose's ball disappeared into the trees, he pulled a *Caddy Shack* with his driver and hurled it toward the trees like an Olympic hammer throw.

Then he stormed over to the golf cart. Pushing me out of the way, he got behind the wheel and took off like the boogeyman was after us. We left Cooter running after our vapor trail. I heard Coot yell, "Hold on, partner!"

Moose was blind with rage as he drove past where his ball had gone into the trees. Risking personal safety, I let go with my good hand and pointed across Moose's chest and said, "It's over there."

Moose turned the cart to that direction like it was on a string. I am not sure if he got up on two wheels or not. As soon as the cart started to turn, I went airborne. Before I even hit the ground, I could hear Cooter laughing from one hundred yards away. He told me later I looked like a cartoon character shot out of a cannon. When I hit the ground, I tucked and rolled to protect myself.

My right vocal cord was paralyzed shut and sometimes made it hard for me to breathe. Talking was especially hard because I would say a few words and then had to wheeze to get a breath.

When I laughed, if you did not know me, you might think I was struggling to breathe. Which in reality I was, but it was not to the point of being in danger.

This incident shook Moose up so bad, and immediately the most horrible thought raced through his mind: How was he going to tell my mother how he had killed her son because he was having a bad day on the golf course? He stopped the cart and got out and ran over to me with fear in his eyes. I was laughing so hard I could not get a breath, and it scared Moose to death. He got down on his knees and put a hand on top of my head. Before he started praying for me, he looked at Cooter and yelled, "Get an ambulance!"

When he started praying, I really thought I might die. I wanted to tell him that I was all right, but I was laughing so hard that was all I could do. Cooter finally got there and asked Moose, "What are you doing?"

Moose said, "My God, I killed him!"

Cooter said, "He is laughing."

Finally I was able to contain myself for a moment; I opened my eyes and saw Moose's horrified expression. As soon as I saw his face, I asked, "Did you find your ball?"

Then I cracked up again. Moose was cussing both of us as he walked back to his truck, and he did not say anything on the way home. It took twenty years for him to see the humor in that game of golf.

It was a bright, sunny day when I drove up to Commerce. I was thinking that in a way, this would be a fresh start for me, which was exactly what I needed. While I was at Kilgore College, I had smoked marijuana with people and drank with the football players. Even after the unbelievable evil I felt when I had my accident, I still worried about fitting in more than pleasing God. Coming into Commerce, I could see the high-rise dormitory where my friend Vance Hale lived.

Commerce, Texas, was only fifty miles from where I had grown up, but it was almost like being in another state. The ground was so flat, and there were hardly any trees to speak of. What few trees there were looked more like little shrubs lined up along a fence line to hide overgrown grass.

I turned my truck into the parking lot of the high-rise and immediately saw Vance's truck pulling out of the parking lot. Some guy that I did not know was driving, so I rolled my window down and held my hand out to stop him. The big blond-haired guy driving said, "You must be the infamous Scooter Drew."

I smiled at this friendly giant and said, "Guilty as charged."

He then extended his massive arm out of the truck window to shake my hand. As I took the big, meaty hand, he said, "Nice to meet you, bro. My name is John Varnell."

Then I asked my huge, new friend, "Is that Vance's truck?"

He shook his head and said, "Yes, it is. He is waiting on you in room 801."

I asked, "Where are you going?"

John said, "We're out of drinks. I'll be back in a few minutes."

Waiving I said, "See you in a few."

As I pulled around behind around behind the high-rise to park, I was thinking a fresh start might be harder than I thought. This building was going to be hard for me to live in. If I parked in a handicapped parking place and used the ramp, it was about a two-hundred-foot walk just to get to the door. If I parked close to the doors, there were twelve steps with no hand rail to contend with.

By the time I made it inside the building and was able to get an elevator, John was back from the store and had caught up with me. I had waited until I could catch an elevator by myself, and as the door was closing, a big hand reached in and stopped it. He bellowed, "Vance said you were slow."

The door opened, and there was two hundred and ninety-five pounds of John Varnell with the biggest, friendliest smile I had seen in a long time. He stepped into the elevator and picked me up into a bear hug and said, "I've heard so much about you."

In a whisper, I replied, "I can't breathe."

John kissed me on the cheek and sat me down and said, "Heard you were a whiner too."

When we got up to Vance's room, John threw open the door and yelled, "Here's Johnny." Then he said, "And look who is with me."

My old friend got up and came rushing over to me and put his arms around me. Vance said, "It's not Kilgore. But we'll have fun."

I hugged my big friend hard and said, "It looks like a concentration camp."

Vance told me, "It's really not that bad. I'll introduce you around."

Then he told me, "Dexter and Hoppy can't wait to see you."

I looked around and asked, "Where are they?"

He pointed out his window to smaller prisonlike buildings across the street and said, "They live in West Halls."

I asked, "Why aren't they over here?"

Vance looked over his shoulder toward West Halls and said, "You know Joseph, when I told him you were on the way, he fired up the grill."

Joseph and Dexter Harvey had both been good friends at Kilgore and were inseparable friends themselves. Dexter was an all-American defensive end who was chiseled from head to toe. Joseph Hopkins was a deadly fast, wide receiver who hated to work out, but loved to grill. He would actually light the grill to cook bologna.

I started to sit down to rest, and Vance asked, "What are you doing?"

Thinking it was obvious, I said, "I need to rest."

Pleading Vance said, "They are waiting on you."

Knowing the futility of resisting, I started back to my truck.

We drove over in Vance's truck so I could just ride and get to know the campus. Some of these West Hall buildings have had entrances that faced the parking lot, but others were built so that there would be a courtyard and the entrances opened up into the courtyard. When Vance parked his truck, I asked, "So where is the door?"

He said, "It's around on the other side."

Then I asked, "Why don't you park down at the end so I don't have to walk so far?"

As he got out, he said, "Get your lazy tail out of the truck."

As I got out, I asked, "So when I get down there? How much farther is it?"

As Vance walked away, he said, "I'm going to tell them we're here."

I yelled, "How will I know where to go?"

As I was slowly walking to the end of the building, I was trying to convince myself that this place would not be so bad. I watched my feet with fevered intensity when I walked; if I didn't, I would fall. I'm slowly moving along when I hear Dexter say, "I thought you'd be faster by now."

I looked up to see my muscular friend standing there and said, "And I thought you would have gotten rid of some of that fat by now."

He said, "Crazy white boy."

As he walked away, I asked, "How will I find y'all?"

Never looking back, he said, "We'll be the ones sitting around the grill."

UNIVERSITY

Vance was right; it was not Kilgore, but it was not bad either. I made friends quick, and soon everyone wanted to be around me. I moved in a West Hall unit that was close to a handicap parking space and once again got a unit to myself. Each apartment had two bedrooms with two beds each, a living area, a kitchenette, and a bathroom.

Going to school here was not the fresh start that I thought it was going to be. I had all these new friends pulling me in different directions, and I was still worried about fitting in. Vance introduced me to Jimmy Cole, and the party was on. Jimmy was a football player from Groveton, Texas, and was country as a chicken coop. I referred to Jimmy as Uncle Jim because he was always taking care of me.

In my first semester, I had a computer science class with more people in than I ever tried to count. One night after class, these two ladies walked up as I was getting my things together. This lady politely asked, "Are you Scooter?"

I said, "Yes, ma'am."

She looked at her friend and said, "This is the boy we used to see walking on the parallel bars."

Jimmy worked as a bartender at a local night club, and I don't think I paid for a drink the whole time I lived in Commerce. Uncle Jim had a race car, and we were always going to drag races—that is, when we weren't fishing. My buddy from high school was also going to school in Commerce, and I introduced him to Jimmy.

Alan Bullock was a country boy in the first degree, and that was enough for Jimmy to love him. We were all fishing one day, and Jimmy caught this tiny bass. Jimmy wanted to take this predatory fish and put it in a fish tank at his girlfriend's house. Ann and her sister Julia had hundreds of angel fish in an eighty gallon tank.

We dropped Jimmy off, and Alan looked at me and said, "Scooter, that bass is going to eat every fish in that tank."

Early the next morning, the phone rang, and it was Jimmy. He was trying to be quiet but was laughing hysterically when he told me, "My bass ate all but about twenty." Laughing hard, he said, "He's so fat he's sitting on the bottom of the tank and can't move."

Astonished I asked, "What are you going to do?'

Cole said, "I don't know, but they are getting up."

I told him, "Get away from the tank."

Then I told him, "They'll notice the fish gone." I was impressed when he said, "They need to know."

We talked two more minutes before the screaming started. Ann and Julia were both screaming, and Jimmy was laughing like crazy. This went on for several minutes, and twenty years later, it still cracks me up.

One afternoon, I was sitting up near the middle of the stadium watching football practice. It was a windy March day, and I had a jacket and a hoodie on to keep warm. Wes Smith was down on the field passing the ball around with the receivers. He had been released from the St. Louis Cardinals after his second season. Wes was cocky with good reason, and I had quickly grown to appreciate him.

From the middle of the field where he was throwing the ball, Wes spotted me sitting way up in the stadium and waved at me.

Wes took a couple of more passes and threw the ball back to Mike Trigg, the Lions all-conference quarterback. Then he turned and jogged over to the track. He came up to where I was sitting and put the hood on his sweatshirt up and said, "It's cold up here."

I was hunkered down and bundled up and said, "It's not cold."

Wes walked over and as he placed the back of his hand on my face said, "Oh yeah."

I pushed his hand away and asked, "What do you want?"

Wes said, "I thought you weren't cold."

I gave him an incredulous look and told him, "I just don't want your nasty hand on my face."

Getting serious, he said, "I have something I want to ask you."

Emphatically I said, "Just don't touch me again!"

Then Wes said, "Trigg told me that you were some hotshot softball manager."

Proudly I said, "I've coached some winning teams."

Wes said, "Why don't you manage us."

Then he said, "I am turning the roster in today."

Regretfully I told him, "Vance asked me to manage his fraternity team."

Wes asked, "Are you going to manage the Phi Kappa Geeka?"

I hated to say this, but I said, "They suck." Continuing the assault, I said, "They don't listen to anything I tell them." Finally exposing some of my face, I asked, "What is the name of our team?"

With a slight smile, he said, "We are the Prototypes."

The Prototypes were good, probably better overall than the Drillers. With the Drillers, every player on the team could slap the ball out the park. The very first tournament that we played in off-the-campus tournament, Cooter hit a leadoff home run. As the ball flew off his bat, he yelled, "Leave here!"

As he stepped on home plate, James Latham threw an M-60 firecracker over the backstop. Hoppy was the smallest guy on the team and hit the most home runs. Those old men looked at one another like, "What did we get into with these guys?"

The Prototypes did not have that kind of power, but they were naturals. The Prototypes were good enough that we won a state title. Mike Trigg played first base and had a very good batting average and was more of the manager than me. He more or less consulted with me on things like the batting order and the hottest fraternity girl sitting in the stands. If I wanted to make an order change, I told Trigg, and he sat them down for me. I watched Wes stand at the left field fence, catch a fly ball, and then throw out a runner trying to score from third base—with a softball, mind you. He had a bionic arm.

The third baseman played tight end on the football team. His real name was Richie Rich, and he was a comedian about everything. I have a very distinguishable voice because of my paralyzed vocal cord. Everybody and their dog imitated me, but Richie could make people think I was talking. He would get me into trouble whenever he could.

Jeff Priest was not a football player, but he talked more trash than anyone on the team. He had this wobble slop pitch that everyone could hit, but no one could get a hold of. The outfielders on our team didn't see much action, but they were all stars. The most fun for the Prototypes was talking trash to the frat boys. Going in to the bottom of the last inning in the championship game of the intramural tournament, we were getting beat.

As my players left the field to bat, the entire ballpark start's chanting, "P, K, A…"

When Wes stepped on home plate to score the winning run, he gave everyone the signal to join him chanting, "P, K, A…"

Rather than celebrating our win, we gloried in their loss.

RAMBO

I had decided that I wanted to be a special education teacher and had started taking education classes. There were the most amazing women on campus in the special education classes with me. My favorite teacher in the Psychology/Special Education Department was Dr. Fullwood.

Dr. Fullwood's classes were always so full, and I would be the only male in the class. While I was still in Kilgore, the guys made me feel guilty about using the electric scooter. We actually put a For Sale sign on it and put it out on the curb and sold it. This campus was so much bigger than the campus in Kilgore. It was a very long walk from the handicapped parking spaces in front of the Psychology/Special Education Building to my classes. It was so long that in my break between classes, I would just hang out in the department office and talk to Ms. Barb.

One day after a football game, I was walking to my truck when this very pretty lady approached me and introduced herself to me. Mrs. Reba Eisenhower told me, "We have heard so much about you from Coach Vowel."

I said to her, "I hope it's not all bad."

Mrs. Eisenhower told me, "You know Eddie loves you." Then she added, "We want to take you to the West Texas State game with us out in Canyon."

Thinking that was really nice, I asked, "Is that a far drive?"

Mrs. Eisenhower said, "Oh, there's no way we could drive. We have to fly."

I was wondering if I could come up with the money for that, so I asked, "How much are the tickets?"

Reba said, "We already have your ticket."

It was hard to believe that these people who did not know me could be so nice to me. I was so excited that we were going to fly out to Canyon, Texas, on the same plane with team that in the weeks leading up to the game it was all I could think or talk about.

On the actual day of the game, we drove to DFW Airport in the Eisenhower's car. Mr. Eisenhower got a man who worked at the airport to take me from the car to the plane in a wheelchair. This was really a big deal for me because it was the first time that I had ever flown. The atmosphere on the plane was a lot of fun. I got to sit in 1st class, and everyone was after me to get them drinks.

The stadium in Canyon was amazing because it was a bowl that was carved out of a mountainside. At the back of the end zones, were these steep grass hills that rose up to the level of the press box. The male West Texas State cheerleaders were walking a buffalo at the back of the end zone while the teams were warming up. Trigg was trying to come back from a knee operation, and I was down on the field talking to him.

Royce Selecta had been the quarterback in Trigg's absence. Royce was a character to the tenth degree. He played second base on the Prototypes and was the only one on the team with a better arm than Wes Smith. Royce walked over to where Mike and I were talking and said, "Scoot, go deep."

I looked at the back of the end zone to where they were leading the buffalo and asked Royce, "Can you hit that buffalo?"

He grinned and asked me, "Do you want me to hit it in the head or the butt?"

Smiling, Trigg said, "Don't hurt it. Hit him in the butt."

Royce took an imaginary snap and, with just a three-step drop, launched the ball over the heads of the West Texas State Buffalos. The pass thrown over the heads of the opposing team as they were warming up drew just about every eye in the stadium. When the football hit that buffalo in the rear flank, he charged up that grassy hill like Theodore Roosevelt and the Rough Riders. The really funny part was that he was dragging all those male cheerleaders behind. Why they did not let go, we'll never know.

At half-time, the Buffalos were beating us thirty-five to nothing. I made my way to the locker room and caught the end of Coach Vowel's verbal assault on the team. As he walked past me on his way out, Coach Vowel said, "They are all yours, Scooter."

You could have heard a pin drop when I asked them, "Are you going to give up?"

I was trying to look every one of them in the eye as I continued, "Getting beat is not that bad. Every team is going to get beat at some point." Knowing I had their attention, I said, "If you give up now, it will make it that much easier the next time." I looked around the locker room into the eyes of my friends when I said, "Coach Vowel has given up on you. Do you see any coaches in here with us?"

A few of them shook their heads no, and I asked, "When have you ever seen that at half-time of a conference game?"

Vance said, "Never."

Then I told them, "They have given up on their ability to inspire you, but you are all men with the ability to inspire yourselves."

Some of them were in tears when I told them what it was like to be paralyzed and the only good thing you had left was your will. I told them, "When you take the field in the second half, don't will to make this a good game or play your best." Some of the team had been staring at the floor until now. With every eye in the locker room on me, I said, "Go out there and will to win."

My friend Mike Trigg got the start in the second half. The Buffalos did not score another point, and in the greatest comeback I have ever seen, we won the game. On the plane ride home, Coach Vowel asked me to travel to all the games.

There was a man in the building next to me who was in one of those big electric wheelchairs that I wished I had. Sometimes in the cafeteria, we would sit together and talk. Jim was a Vietnam veteran and had been injured driving an eighteen-wheeler and was always great to talk with. My time at that university would have been so much easier if I would have had an electric wheelchair myself. Jim White played chess, and we would get together all the time and play. Jim was also a quadriplegic, only he never had all the return that I had. He wore hand splints and could only do a few things with his fingers. Between the two of us knocking pieces over, we spent most of our time setting the board back up. His attendant, Carol Smith, was a dead ringer for Kareem Abdul Jabbar.

Carol and I decided we were going to take a homemaking class as an elective together. The first day of the class, we were walking in right at the bell. We were crossing over to the other side of the room to the only vacant seats when the teacher exclaimed, "I know you!"

Then she said, "You're the guy who locked me in the office when I was student teaching."

Her face dropped when she said, "What happened to you?"

When I was a junior, I had a homemaking class with five of my friends whom I played football with. We were most definitely any student teacher's nightmare. We got this student teacher whom we were all infatuated with; that was the only reason we gave her any respect at all.

The homemaking cottage had an office with glass walls, but for some reason, the door locked from the outside. One morning in class, Mitzie Hawkins, our student teacher, was sitting at a table by herself studying one of her textbooks. Ricky Wells said, "That girl is neglecting our education."

Sam Morris said, "If she were over here, you wouldn't be paying attention."

Terry Drennan said, "The point is, she is not doing her job."

I jumped in and said, "Yeah, but look at her."

Ken Bradshaw looked at me and said, "Stop being a slut."

Jerry Pinnell asked, "Do y'all want to get out of class?"

Jerry was widely known for plans that got us all in trouble. When he graduated, he passed that torch to me. Jerry went on to say, "One of us will make up an excuse to go to the office."

Jerry said, "When you get to the office, you call the cottage, and when she answers the phone, we lock her in the office and leave."

Ken said, "I got this one."

Then he turned to Mitzie and said, "I stepped on a nail and left my antibiotics at home. Can I go to the office and pick them up?"

He finished this remarkable lie by saying, "My mom dropped them off for me."

I looked across the table at Ken and said, "That was a good one."

Terry hit me under the table and said, "Be quiet."

As Ken headed out of the door of the cottage, Jerry asked, "Who is going to lock her in the office?"

Everyone sitting at the table turned to look at me, and I asked, "Why have I got to do it?"

Sam told me, "No one will be surprised if you do it."

About that time, the phone rang, and Mitzie said, "One of you get that please."

I told her, "We are not allowed to go into the office for any reason."

As she answered the phone, I shut the office door and locked it. As we were leaving the cottage, we all waved good-bye to a hysterical student teacher.

Back over at the high school, we are drinking Cokes in the foyer laughing and have a good time. Mr. Talbert walked out of his office and put his hands on his hips then said, "Get over there and let that poor girl out of the office."

Then he said, "She just called me in tears." As we were leaving, he said, "Scooter, this is not over."

I saw these posters around campus advertising the coming up student elections. I figured with all the friends that I had, I would be a shoe in for any position that I ran for. I went to the office to get on the ballot to run for president. Because I had never been on the senate, I could only run for vice president. To my surprise, there was actually a monthly salary for vice president. I ran out of gas so many times that Uncle Jim carried a gas can in his truck with gas in it. Anything that they paid would be a big help.

The incumbent president was running for reelection, and his best friend was running for vice president. They put their suits on every day and got out and walked the campus campaigning. My campaign was limited to just telling all of my friends to vote for me.

After the election, Vance came to my West Hall room and told me, "Voting for vice president was close enough for a run off."

Disappointed I said, "I thought I would run away with it."

Sarcastically Big V said, "I guess you should have campaigned some. You have one week to finally campaign."

The night before the runoff, we made some campaign posters and put them out while even the most notorious night owls were sleeping. On the actual day of the election, I stayed at the university student center talking to people and getting them to vote. Three hours before the polls closed, I was exhausted. Vance came walking by on the way to check his mail and said, "Hey, how's it going?"

I asked him, "Have you voted yet?"

He smiled and said, "I voted this morning."

The next day, I found out I lost the runoff by one vote. Just like the old fable about the race between a rabbit and a turtle, overconfidence lost the election for me. I had gone to Vance's room about two hours before the polls closed to hang out and played spades with the team. That night, I was sitting in the cafeteria with Joseph Hopkins and Dexter eating dinner. They were trying to be encouraging after my big disappointment.

We are sitting there eating when these Pike pledges came walking by. Finally, a smile came over my face when I saw these guys with their pants rolled up to their knees and the bills of their caps pressed back. Dexter watched me smiling and reached over and poked Hoppy on the arm.

Dexter said, "You know you want to get up there with those peckerwoods."

I looked at him and said, "They are ridiculous."

Dexter and Hoppy were both Phi Beta Sigma. African American fraternities have a completely different view of what a pledge period should be like. Their fraternity pledges did not go through a hell week, but six weeks of hell.

Dexter said, "You couldn't handle our frat."

Then Hoppy said, "You would drop in the first week."

I never wanted to be in a fraternity, but I said, "When do I start?"

That night, the Sigma big brothers met to discuss including me on their next line when it started. It was called a line because the line brothers all had new names and went everywhere in a line. We lined up from shortest to tallest. I was the tallest and was at the end of the line, so my line name was White Shadow. They never made me quit, but after the pledge period, I was through with frat life. I had only done it to prove to Dexter and Joseph that I could.

One thing that kept giving me trouble to no end was college algebra. With the head injury that I had, my psychologist told me that anything with abstract concepts was going to give me trouble. It was so frustrating to work so hard at something and not be able to get it.

School was fun for me, but just like in high school, application to school work was not one of my strong points. It seemed like there was always something to keep my mind from my studies. The biggest thing that seemed to distract me was Angela Corrigan. The room where I moved into was in that same quad where Dexter and Joseph lived, only I found a turn around on the other side that had handicapped parking.

Angela lived in the building next to mine, and until I had a class with her, we never said more than a few words to each other. She had a dark tan and long, blond, curly hair, with long legs and eyes that could melt the coldest heart. One of the psychology classes that were required for me was Psychology of Sexual Behavior.

The first day of class, I came in and took a seat by the door. Just before the bell rang, Angela came walking in, and though there were empty seats all over, she sat down right beside me. After she had taken her seat, she looked at me and said, "Hey, neighbor."

Trying to contain myself, I said, "I am going to fail this class."

She asked, "Why do you say that?

I looked at her longingly and said, "You."

Then she said, "Oh no, you are my study partner." To really drive me crazy, she said, "I study in lingerie."

I knew that I had an angel on my shoulder because all my cool football player friends could not even get the time of day from her. The first night I went to her apartment to study, for a joke she answered the door in a blue, silk teddy. I staggered back and fell off the porch. Richard McCullom walked around the corner and saw her bending down over me. Richard leaned down, looked at me, smiled, and then said, "Do you even want up?"

Richard was a linebacker and a cage fighter back when it was first getting started. We were so much alike and were always together. I still worked out with the team and was in the weight room the day he squatted eight hundred and eighty pounds. I used to go with him to fights and be his corner man—not that he needed one. I never saw one of his fights go to the second round. Richard was like me in that he had had a troubled life. He was there on scholarship money and nothing else. He did not have any support from anyone. That's why he fought. It came down to selling drugs, stealing, or fighting.

Everyone called Richard Rambo, except for me and his girlfriend. One day he comes to me and says, "We have to come up with the gas money to get to Oklahoma City this weekend."

I asked, "Are we going up there to fight?"

As he held up a vial of testosterone, he said, "What do you think?"

Then he asked, "Will you shoot me?"

I replied, "Yeah, if you draw it up."

Richard would go to these fights raging on steroids and annihilate everyone he fought—that is, until Oklahoma City. He fought his way easily into the championship fight and was set to face the black Chuck Norris. I told Richard that his only chance to beat this guy was to take him to the ground and squeeze the life out of him. Well, this man had been watching Richard fight too.

Richard met him at center ring, and they received instructions then shook hands. As soon as the karate man let go of Richard's hand, he jumped up and spun around and kicked my friend on the jaw with the heel of his foot. Blood shot out of Richard's mouth and flew across the ring like a super soaker water gun had sprayed it. He staggered a little, but he never went down. After he got stabilized, he shook his head and looked at me and yelled, "Throw the towel in!"

I yelled back, "You can beat this guy!"

Richard ran over, and I held the towel out behind my back. For a few seconds, I managed to hold the towel out of his reach. Finally, he grabbed me by the collar and pulled me into the ring. Then he took the towel out of my hand and turned around and handed it to the referee. The next week before practice, Richard walked into the field house drinking beer, and Coach Vowel kicked him off the team. He came and said good-bye, and just like that, he was gone. Richard came to visit once after that. I had been out late with Uncle Jim and never heard him knocking on the door. I woke up to him crawling through my bedroom window. It was a snowy day during Christmas break and we got out and hit those deserted back roads around Commerce and talked a lot. We found this old barn with an open loft and a snow covered tin roof that looked so cool that we had to investigate. We got high in that barn and Rambo prayed and accepted Jesus as his savior. That was the last time I ever saw him.

DROP OUT

One day after sex class, Angela walked me to the office. She was helping me get my backpack off so I could sit down when Dr. Fullwood came in. Dr. Fullwood stood there looking at Angela like she was naked. When I sat down, she kissed me on top of my head and said, "I'll see you tonight."

I just said, "Bye, babe."

She was not even out of earshot when he asked me, "How in the world do you it?"

Smiling I asked, "Do what?"

He said, "You know exactly what I am talking about."

Dr. Ball was one of my psychology professors and someone whom I considered a friend. He looked at Dr. Fullwood and said, "I know exactly what he does."

Turning to face him, Dr. Fullwood said, "Enlighten me, Steve."

Dr. Ball said, "Well, Harry, girls don't feel threatened with Scooter."

Dr. Fullwood said, "They don't know him like I do then."

I looked at Dr. Ball and said, "That's good. I know I don't have anything to offer a woman, and I don't try to get in their pants." Looking down the hall where Angela had just departed, I said, "I am scared to death of her."

Dr. Fullwood said, "That girl thinks the world of you."

Still watching Angela walk away, I said, "So does my mother."

Dr. Ball said, "Scooter, you have more heart than anyone I know, and that, my friend, is what women are looking for."

I looked up and said, "Dr. Ball, I can barely walk, and there are times I can't even make it to the bathroom. If I found a girl to go out with me, I'd have to take her to my room to watch television. Angela sees me like a best friend." Looking at Dr. Fullwood, I said, "No one wants to be with a dirt-poor, crippled man."

Dr. Fullwood's jaw dropped, and his eyes began to well up, and he said, "Son, I want you to listen to me closely. People who own everything they ever wanted wish they had what you have."

Dr. Ball said, "I sure do."

Dr. Fullwood continued, "I watch you with people and listen to the way people talk about you, and I am so proud of you."

Dr. Ball added, "You make me proud every day."

Then I said, "I know I have a lot of friends. What I need is a job."

Dr. Fullwood asked, "If I got you on as a substitute at the elementary school, could you handle all the walking?"

Before I even asked, deep down I knew that I could not hold up to all the walking. What would the kids think the first time I had a wet spot because I couldn't get to the bathroom on time? I asked Dr. Fullwood, "What would I have to do to be able to substitute?"

Dr. Fullwood said, "Nothing to it, just pass a background check."

This horrible thought went through my head as I asked, "What are they looking for?"

Dr. Ball said, "Mainly just felonies."

Then I asked, "How far back do they go?"

Dr. Ball asked, "Scooter, is there something you want to tell us?"

I said, "I got a felony my senior year in high school."

Both of them at the same time asked, "For what!"

I found out two things sitting in the office that day. The first thing that I learned that day was that many people wished they could make friends as easily as me. The second thing was I would never be able to teach school because of a felony on my record. Walking out of the psychology department that day, there was a huge hole in my heart. The last two and a half years had been a huge waste because of all the education classes that I had taken. Never in my wildest imaginations had the thought that they would hold something against me that happened before my accident.

I got to my truck and just sat there wondering what I was going to do. What kind of job could I get in the condition that my body was in? The handicapped parking spaces were right in front of the campus infirmary. I sat there watching students go in and then come out again. I must have sat there in shock and disbelief for three hours thinking about what I was going to do.

One of my old cattle-rustling buddies from high school had a business in Mesquite, and maybe he could find something for me to do. Carl Nelson had gone to work selling Kirby vacuum cleaners after high school and had worked his way into a distributorship. I called Carl and set up a time for us to go to lunch together, thinking maybe some way I could sell vacuum cleaners.

The only person whom I told about my plans to leave was Angela, and she was not for it at all. Carl had been thinking about expanding his business into two teams with two sales managers for a while. With me needing a job gave him the opportunity to do that, because he knew that he could train me to succeed. I would commute from Commerce to Mesquite until I had the money to move to Mesquite. While I was being trained by Carl's sales manager during the day, I set appointments in the phone room at night.

At first I got an apartment on Scyene Road in Mesquite. It was not that far from where Carl's office was. I was given a sales team to manage and oversee. You put ten different personalities in the field with all of their eccentricities and quirks, and a closer's job is never done.

Every day I would get to the office around seven thirty, and I'd be lucky to get to go home by nine thirty. Even then I was not through closing the evening sales, and I had to be ready any minute to take a call and close a sale.

One night, I was sitting in Red Lobster with friend having dinner with him and his three kids. There was a party on the other side of this divider that was celebrating a birthday. There were at least twenty people in the party, and they were so loud.

Mike Bloom was one of my best salesmen, and he was always on an eight o'clock appointment. One of the requirements about a salesperson on a preset appointment was that they check in when they got there. When the demo was done, they were to call in for a phone close. The Mormon Tabernacle Choir was warming up for another a rousing rendition of "Happy Birthday" when my phone rang. Mike said, "Mr. Drew, this is Mike Bloom, and I just got to the Alexander's home."

I asked, "How does everything look?"

Under his breath, Mike said, "Jimmy, this is a beautiful home."

I replied, "Well, pull a lot of rags and create value."

Mike answered and said, "I doubt there is any dirt in this house to pull on a rag."

At that moment, a manager appeared at our table and said, "Excuse me, sir."

I told Mike, "Buddy, do your best and call me before you leave."

I put my phone down and asked, "What is it, sir?"

He told me, "The people on the other side say that your phone is bothering them."

At that exact moment, they yelled so loud that everyone in the restaurant looked in their direction. I asked the manager, "Did you hear that?"

He said, "I know, sir. They complained, so I had to say something."

I said, "Tell them their singing is disturbing my phone calls."

He smiled and asked, "Do you really want me to?"

I said, "Absolutely."

At that exact moment, my phone rang again. Carl Esco was a good friend from Kilgore College, and he and his children were having dinner with me. Carl said, "Let it ring a few times."

I looked at my phone and said, "It is one of my salespeople. It can go to voice mail."

As soon as the phone stopped ringing, I sent Leah a text message and told her to call me right back.

My phone goes to voice mail after the fifth ring, so I answered on the fourth ring. Leah said, "Hey, Mr. Drew, I am at the Simpson home, and I am getting ready to show them the new Kirby."

I asked her, "Ms. Leah, can you do me a favor?"

She said, "Sure, Jimmy."

Then I said, "Call me right back."

She said, "Sure."

In just a few seconds, the phone rang again four times, and I answered and said, "Thanks, Leah."

Just then this man appeared around the partition and said, "If I hear that phone again or that raspy voice of yours, there is going to be a problem."

Carl played tight end at Kilgore and then finished up his eligibility at a university in Oklahoma. There are not very many two-hundred-and-sixty-pound receivers that can move the way Carl could. Carl stood up and said, "If I see your ugly, honky face again, there is going to be a problem. Now are we going to have a problem?"

I closed sales and did contracts with Mike and Leah that night, and we never heard another word from birthday boy.

I got tired of living in an apartment complex and began to look for a place of my own that I could afford. I found a place that I liked and went to see my old friend Jan Wilkinson. Carl had long since sold out of the Kirby Business and I had gone to work for SBC. I started out selling advertisement for the white pages. Within the first month I was leading the company in conversions. Jan was now Jan Mills, and she was the president of First National Bank in Winnsboro. Jan helped me out, and I was a first-time homeowner. The neighborhood that I moved to was at Stephens Park in the Oak Cliff area. The really weird thing was it was only five blocks from the place where I was born. Stephens Park Hospital had been torn down, but I was back. I did not know that I was born in this neighborhood until the first time Mom came to visit.

It was my first Saturday morning in my new house, and I decided I was going to go for a walk to check out my neighbors. A walk for me consisted of walking a hundred feet and then resting for two or three minutes. After an hour, I was only about three blocks from my house and getting very tired. I was looking for a place to sit down when I heard someone yell, "Scooter Drew."

I looked in the direction the voice came from and saw this man with long hair running toward me. As he came closer, I asked, "Bengie?"

He stopped running, and he and threw his arms around me and pulled me into a hug. Putting his mouth close to my ear, he whispered, "No one has called me Bengie in a long time."

This was Clint Hooks little brother. I played football with Clint, and they grew up about a quarter of a mile down the highway from me. That's almost next-door neighbors when you live in the country. During the time that I lived in the neighborhood, Ben had two sons. They both would run to me with books in their hands whenever I came over. From me reading to them, they were both reading by the time they started kindergarten.

One afternoon I came home from work early because I was not feeling well, and as I opened the front door, empty spaces caught my eye. There was an empty space where my television had been. There was a big, empty space on my desk where my computer had been. There were lots of other empty spaces too. I called the police first thing, and they sent the special burglary unit out. Not.

This lady officer came and dusted for fingerprints. She did not find any—not even mine. She told me the only place you could find a print was on a flat, glass surface. Apparently, she never watched *CSI*. I had just spent five months writing a novel. The disk that it was saved on was in that computer.

The next day, Ben called me and told me he had something for me, and he said he would be there in just a minute with it. When he pulled in to my yard, I see this big black chow in his front seat. Ben opened his door and stepped out, and this dog got behind him and ran out in the middle of my yard and rutted his hind feet like an angry bull. Then he trotted up on the porch and went to the door to be let in. I did not have a fence, and Ben left a thirty-foot logging chain for me to let him outside on.

I named him Boseman after this tattoo artist friend of ours. A few days after I got him, he would not let anyone touch him but me. Ben builds custom choppers and rides; so one weekend, we're all gearing up to go to a motorcycle rally in a small city of West Texas. All of the supplies were loaded in my Blazer, and my dog was in the passenger seat. Danny Boseman is six foot six and covered in tattoos. He is not at all heavy for his height, but he is as big as a barn door. Danny walked up to my side window and said, "What are you going to name him?"

I replied, "Boseman."

Looking at my dog, Danny just said, "He is scary."

Danny did a tattoo of an angel with a cane on my left bicep that even other tattoo artists have told me is great work. The really funny thing is Danny was the only man that Boseman ever let touch him without getting bit. Ben was there all the time but he never put a finger on him.

If he wasn't on that chain when I let him out, he would kill every animal that would not run from him. If you were in my house and made a sudden movement, he was all over you. I only let him out on the chain so there would be no dead animals proudly laid on my porch in the morning.

After work, I would walk to Ben's house for exercise. After years of walking, my hips and knees began to bother me really bad. One night while walking home from Ben's house, I walked into my driveway and my hip was hurting so bad I thought I cracked it the day before in a fall. I barely made it inside and fell on my living room floor. Thinking my hip must be broken, I dialed 911.

Before the ambulance got to my house, I opened the door and let Boseman outside to terrorize the neighborhood. If he were in the house, there would be no way an EMT could touch me to give me help. As they closed the doors on the ambulance, I saw that my front door was wide open. I asked the EMT who had climbed in the back of the ambulance with me, "Will someone close my door?"

While getting an IV started, he said, "Don't worry about that, partner."

My hip was not cracked, but the joints were so eroded from osteoarthritis that the doctor said I needed a double-hip replacement. Which I never took the time to get done. Early the next morning, I called Mom to see if she could go to my house and round up Boseman. If there were any outside pets left alive in my neighborhood, they were stuck up in a tree somewhere.

When Mom got to the hospital, she asked, "Did you drive yourself up here?"

Not understanding, I said, "Mom, I told you I came by ambulance."

Before she could say anything else I asked, "Did you find my dog?"

Mom said, "Stop worrying, he was sitting on the porch when I got there."

Then she asked, "Where is your Blazer?"

Thinking this could not be true, I said, "It better be in my driveway."

Mom said, "Well, it is not."

This time the 911 operator answered the phone the exact same way, "911 emergency, what is your emergency?"

Replying with the same monotone voice that she answered with, I said, "I'd like to report my car stolen."

Then as if it were a recorded response, she asked, "What is your name please?"

I answered, "Jimmy Drew."

Next she asked, "What is your date of birth?"

I said, "Eleven fourteen sixty-four."

There was at least a minute of silence before, with some life in her voice, she asked, "What are you trying to pull?"

Angrily I asked, "What did you just say to me?"

As if she were talking to a child, she said, "This is the third time you have called us in twelve hours."

Defiantly, I said, "No, it is not."

She said, "You called once because you thought you broke your hip. Then shortly after that you called because a mad dog had you trapped in the house, and animal control went out."

She tried to continue but I said, "What did you say about a dog?"

She repeated, "You called 911 emergency because a dog had you trapped inside your home."

Then I said, "I'm going to need your supervisor."

The EMTs had left the door to my house open, and someone came inside to search for treasure. However, while they were in the privacy of my home playing pirate, Boseman came home and trapped them inside. The back door had a padlock on it. They had my keys but did not have the brains to try them. There was no way Boseman was going to let them out without chewing some criminal butt. The people robbing my house called the police to help them get away in my car. Later my Blazer was found stripped of the wheels and tires. I was able to recover it from the impound lot without paying any fees because of the Police Department being an accomplice in it being stolen. I tried to no avail to get them to pay for new wheels and tires.

Five years before I had a Bronco stolen from the Town East Mall parking lot. That vehicle was never recovered nor was the allure of Dallas, Texas. One day I was at the Dairy Way convenience store on Jefferson Avenue putting gas in my old Dodge pickup. After the Bronco was stolen I bought it from Ben and used the rest of the insurance towards the down payment on my home. It was an old beat up truck, but it would have run forever. I traded it at a car lot on Fort Worth Avenue for the Blazer.

While I was filling my tank, this 63 Chevy Impala pulls up on the other side of the pumps. Four gang bangers get out and the beauty of a warm spring day turned uneasy as a dirt road to perdition. Three of them were only concentrating on the blunt they were smoking, but the driver had his eyes transfixed on me. The first thing that entered my mind was, *I am about to be part of a gang initiation.*

Sure enough the leader looked at the biggest one of the bunch on the other side of his car and said, "That's him." Then he nodded in my direction. When they pulled up, I reached over into the bed of my truck and got my cane out. Not for protection, but because even gang bangers would not jump a crippled white boy. The big guy that had got the nod started in my direction and

I locked eye contact with him. I was not trying to intimidate him, but I wanted him to see my humanity. I am over six foot and this big man stared down at me like I was a child. I never said a word; I just stood there staring into his eyes.

Finally the driver screamed, "Hit that fool." There was compassion in his eyes and I knew that God was protecting me. After thirty more seconds he turned around and walked back around the car. The owners of the store were four brothers from India. As I climbed into my truck I saw them all standing at the door watching, each of them with a weapon of some sort.

Even though the hospital where I had been born was only a few blocks away, I did not belong here anymore. At this point I did not know if I belonged anywhere. When I first moved to Oak Cliff I was walking in Winn Dixie and car that stopped to let me pass power jacked his engine. I guess this guy thought if he floored the accelerator and rode the breaks to scare a cripple it would be funny. The revving engine and the spinning tires did scare me, but I never looked at the car.

I dropped my cane where I stood and tried to run. Strangely enough I actually cleared the driveway but fell headlong and face first into the curb. Within an hour my left eye was swollen shut and the side of my face was purple for nearly a month. The car drove away expediently to avoid the hostile glares of any bystanders. The gangsters at the store weighed heavy on my decision to sell everything but my clothes and Boseman to Ben and move back to Winnsboro. I left a great job with Southern Bell and left the city.

In the back of my mind, for a long time I had been thinking about finishing my degree and trying to get someone to let me teach. The house that I grew up in burned down two years after my dad died. The year before he died, he had built a nice garage that stood apart from the house. Mom was living and working in Dallas and had no desire to rebuild the house, but I wanted a place to go. I had the garage remodeled into a studio apartment with a laundry room.

It was an honor to live in a structure that my father built before lung cancer claimed his life. My dad was diagnosed with cancer in December, but it was so progressed that he was gone by February. One day I returned to the office from lunch, and Carl was standing in the parking lot waiting for me. His eyes were red, and I knew he had been crying, which was something I had never seen him do before. As I pulled in to my parking space, he approached my window with a serious expression. Rolling down my window, I asked, "What is wrong?"

Carl knew my father well, and when he lowered his face, tears fell from his eyes, and he said, "You need to go to Winnsboro."

My mom had called him, and when he looked up, he said, "Big Jim will not live through the night."

When I arrived home, there were several cars parked in the driveway, and I began to brace myself—for what, I did not know. My father had always been a very big man who received so much respect from everyone who knew him. People did not respect him because he could take his way by force if he wanted to. He received so much respect from people because he gave everyone respect, and he was always fair and kind.

When I walked into the house, there was no one in sight, but I heard voices in my father's bedroom. I stood in the doorway and observed my mother and a few other people around his bed. Dad was in a great deal of pain and had already lost his ability to speak. His eyes were closed, and he was moaning from what must have been unbearable pain.

When I stepped up to his bed, my Mom said, "Honey, look who is here."

Dad opened his eyes and smiled like a young boy and tried to speak. Mom said, "Look at that."

His nurse was there with her and, through her tears, said, "I have never seen anything like that."

Dad had been waiting on me, so I pulled a chair beside his bed and laid my head down on the pillow beside him. He died that night, and sitting next to his body, the first person I called was Vance. Big V was married and had baby boy and lived and worked in the Houston area. Within five hours, he was at my side.

After the funeral, there was a reporter who showed up at our house to get information for my dad's obituary in the paper. Mom was a wreck so I took the reporter into the dining room, which also served as my dad's office. Pulling up a chair to his filing cabinet to see what could be found to help, I was joined my dad's younger brother. My uncle Charlie told me, "Son, look at Jim's service record."

I opened up the air force envelope and sat there in amazement. Dad had told me that he was a nose gunner on a B17, but that was all I knew. My dad's plane had been shot down on one of the many bombing missions behind enemy lines. I looked up at Uncle Charlie and asked, "Why didn't he tell me about all these medals?"

Uncle Charlie answered, "Your dad was the biggest man that I ever knew."

I could live on the old home site and drive sixty miles to school at Texas A&M University-Commerce. I had talked to an advisor and found out that to graduate with a degree in psychology, there were only three classes for me to take. A mere nine hours separated me from a college diploma. One afternoon while in a grocery store, this guy walked up and asked, "Scooter, do you remember me?"

He was definitely from Winnsboro because he had on a Metallica concert T-shirt, Wranglers, roper boots, and a Winnsboro Feed and Seed baseball cap.

He knew I was struggling to place him, so he said, "I am Jerry Rogers's son, Michael Rogers."

Taken by surprise because in twenty years he had actually grown up, I said, "Imagine that."

Then Michael said, "You look great."

Before I could even say thanks, he asked, "What are you about to do?"

I told him, "I need to pick up a few things and then home."

Michael looked at me and, like there nothing else for me to do at that moment that mattered, said, "Follow me I'll show you my new cabin."

Before I even said okay, he said, "We'll go by and see Mama first."

Michael's dad was the only man in Winnsboro whom I knew who was bigger than my dad. They were friends, but Michael was so little the last time I saw him there is no way I could have placed him. However, he looked exactly the same as he did as a kid, only larger. His dad had been a true cowboy and right down to roping and riding. Every time I saw him on a horse, I felt sorry for the horse.

Both of our dads had passed away ten years before, and it was so natural to take up their friendship. The best thing about it was I had finally found a country boy to take me fishing. Michael had a really nice bass boat and promised to take me fishing any time I wanted. One afternoon, we were gearing up to go on a coon hunt that night when I said, "Let's go fishing tonight— me, you, and Penny. Maybe Penny won't be strong enough to help get me in the boat."

Michael cockily replied, "I can get you in the boat."

Disagreeing I said, "Getting me in a boat is hard. Cooter and Moose can barely do it."

Repeating himself he said, "I can get you in the boat."

We decided that we would go fishing at Lake Cypress that night and fish under the bridge for crappie. That night, sitting in the truck, I watched Michael and Penny hitch up the boat. As Penny was opening the back door on the driver's side to get in, I saw Michael putting a stepladder in the back the truck. Before he backed the boat down the ramp, he looked at me and said, "Let's get you in the boat."

When I got out, Michael was grabbing the stepladder out of the back of the truck. He walked around and set the ladder up beside the boat and said, "Get in, I will not let you fall." Then he turned to Penny and said, "Baby, get in the boat and let him hold on to you when he steps in."

Penny looked at me and winked then said, "Do not get fresh."

It worked perfectly, and stepping into the boat I turned and sat down on the other side of the boat. Penny sat in one of the seats in the front, and Michael sat beside me at the steering wheel.

The lake was dark as Michael backed his boat away from the ramp. After he was in deep-enough water, he dropped the motor and hit the throttle. As that bass boat, which at the moment seemed to be all motor, hit open water, we were already at fifty miles per hour. After, few short minutes were needling over seventy miles per hour.

Michael tried to make me think he was going to shoot the bridge at seventy-five-mile per hour in the dark. He shut the throttle down and began a rainbow turn in plenty of time to get it shut down. Not before the thought had crossed my mind to fall over the side of the boat and float until he could return—if he made it safely under and could even return at all. We fished under the bridge and caught several good fish. We had thirty fish at sunrise, and a few of them made a great breakfast. We had fried eggs, biscuits and red-eye gravy, and fried fish for breakfast.

Michael's mom was the manager of the government low-income housing, and she told me she could get me in her Sulphur

Springs Units. If I moved in there, it would knock sixty miles off my commute. Pam juggled the waiting list for me, and Michael moved me into the next available unit. I was living on my own and very comfortably at that. My apartment was decorated very nicely, thanks to Lee and Pam for bringing me pieces that they had picked up here and there. Lee was Michael's younger sister.

My childhood friend Gabe Cordova lived four blocks east of my apartment. Gabe and Robert were the same age, and to say that we had covered some tracks would not be a metaphor. Gabe and the rest of the Cordova clan boiled crawfish every week of the crawfish season. More than likely, Robert was there, and it was almost like old times. In the afternoons, I walked to Gabe's just like I had done with Ben. Just like Ben, Gabe had two sons. Gabe's wife, Carla, grew up in our small town as well. Even though she never stalked the railroad tracks with us, she was country to the bone.

The three hardest classes on my degree plan were statistics, college algebra, and physiology of the brain. It just happened that those were the three classes left on my degree plan before graduation. My last semester in college was spent drowning in a sea of homemade flashcards. Between the medulla oblongata, negative integers, and Z scores, my life was blurred into one textbook and the twenty-mile stretch of Highway 11 between my apartment and the campus.

One morning nearing the semester's end, my car was on autopilot heading into the campus for a meeting with my statistics professor. For a project that was to be a major percentage of our grade, we had been given a set of scores and presented with the tasks of figuring a complete statistical analysis. Before we turned our projects in, Dr. Haung would go over them with us and give us insight on how to improve them.

DÉJÀ VU

I never liked being the teacher's pet, but at the same time, I never failed to take advantage of it. Dr. Haung was from a tiny village in China that was now underwater because of the building of a massive dam. Other students would give her a hard time because she might mispronounce words or have a hard time understanding them. She fascinated me, and we had a very good relationship because of my respect for her. After my call to let her know our meeting would be a little late, Dr. Haung was patiently sitting in her office waiting on me. Coming into Commerce on Highway 11, the road goes from seventy-five miles per hour to fifty-five, and the within another quarter mile, there is a twenty-five-mile-per-hour curve. My eyes were more on my project than on the road, and suddenly my tires were off the road, and the tree at the apex of that curve brought me to a sudden stop.

The crushing force of the crash shattered the windshield and crunched the hood in like a smashed Coke can. The first thing that caught my attention was the fact that my face slamming into the steering wheel had bent it. Then reaching for my seatbelt, there was knock on the driver's-side-door window. A reassuring voice said, "Sir, please, be still."

Looking out my window, the police officer assured me, "An ambulance is on the way."

She could not get the door open, and soon there were firemen there to cut me out. They pulled me out of that car like they were threading a needle. There was an ambulance there almost instantly because the police officer at my window was right behind me when my car went off the road.

The ambulance took me to the emergency room in Commerce. If they did not get that hard board that they had used in the ambulance from under me soon, it did not seem would matter. There was something really wrong, and I could feel my life slipping away. There was a burning pain in my abdomen that felt like a shovel full of hot coals had been dropped inside my stomach. I remember watching nurses attending to me and keeping a steady eye on the heart monitor beside me thinking that line would go flat any second. After all the things that I had overcome and the hundreds of friends who were always there for me, I was dying in a small town emergency room all alone. I watched the monitor go flat, and there was no will left in me to fight.

This time it was totally different from when I broke my neck in high school, because this time there was no fear. I knew that I had passed to the other side and the day to day struggle was over. Emotionally, I was at peace, not knowing what to expect next. Though my life had not been an advertisement for all that Christianity represents, I was going to church every Sunday, and I was the embodiment of a believer.

When the heart monitor went flat, I knew that I closed my eyes for the last time. The next time I opened them, I was sitting at a big, white table in a vast expanse of white. There was a very large man sitting across the table from me. The only thing in my field of vision that was not white were the sandals on the big man's feet. He stoically sat there across from me, not saying a word.

I did not feel fear this time. Sitting there in the presence of an angel, I was ashamed of all the things that I had done just to fit in with the crowd. Though the shame of my actions in my life weighed on my mind, the gentle look on the giant angel's face welcomed me home. There was no pain or aching bones, and the regret of my less-than-perfect life soon faded into hopeful expectancy. Knowing that soon I would see Jesus, there was no desire to go back to the constant struggle of a life filled with pain, poverty, and solitude.

I thought back through all the pain and the many tears and was so happy to be in a place of rest. The man across from me had flowing white hair and a white beard. I sat there looking at him wondering where he was going to take me when he said, "You don't want to go back, do you?"

I replied, "Please do not make me go back."

He answered and said, "The choice is yours."

Leaning forward, he put his hand on my shoulder and said, "Your pain will not last forever."

Again I said to him, "Please do not make me go back."

As he removed his hand, he said, "There will be a lot of people who don't make it if you don't go back."

Then we were not sitting together anymore, and I could see people from all walks of life doing different things, but each of them had no awareness of the others. Somehow I knew that my purpose in life was to make their lives better. These people were lost and had no hope of finding their way without someone telling them my story. In some way, I knew that if I chose to help those people, my suffering had only just begun.

When I opened my eyes, there was a ventilator connected to my throat, and it felt as though my stomach had been removed with a backhoe. I was in a newer facility than the hospital in Commerce where I had been taken by the ambulance. Obviously I was right off the nursing station of an intensive care unit of a hospital, just not the one in Commerce.

A nurse came in to check something and saw that I was awake. She removed a pocket light from the pocket of her blouse and stepped over to look at my eyes. She told me, "Open your eyes wide."

I asked, "Where am I?"

The nurse said, "Mr. Drew, you are in the hospital."

A few minutes later, a doctor stepped into the glass enclosure where I was to examine me. As he looked into my eyes with his light, he said, "Jimmy, I am Dr. Kendrick. You were transported to the hospital in Greenville for your operation. I operated on you yesterday."

Inquisitively I asked, "What did you do?"

Pulling down the sheet, he revealed a row of staples that started five inches above my navel and then disappeared into the Congo. Alarmed, I repeated, "What did you do?"

Dr. Hendricks drew a picture of a circle the size of his fist on my chart and showed me his artwork. Then he said, "When you hit that tree, it threw your body forward with so much force. When your seatbelt stopped you, it ripped a hole in the mesentery the size of this circle."

Then I had to ask, "What is the mesentery?"

He replied, "It is the lining around the stomach."

Next I asked, "Why does my throat hurt so badly?"

My doctor told me, "The seatbelt also crushed your larynx."

Then he said, "We had to perform another tracheotomy on you. Do you remember anything?"

I answered, "I just took my eyes off the road."

His eyes had been on my chart, but he looked at me and said, "You know what I mean. I watched you bleed to death internally." As he examined the incision on my abdomen, he went on, "People who lose as much blood as you lost die even after they have it put back in them. Do you remember anything?"

I asked, "Like what?"

Another nurse walked in with a vial of medicine for my intravenous bag, and Dr. Kendrick said, "We'll talk later, I need to know." Before he walked away, he said, "I want to know what you saw."

I was not sure what to tell him. After the first experience when I was in the presence of the devil I had doubts about whether it had actually happened or not. I thought that maybe in my fear I imagined it and conjured it up from stories that I had heard. Even though I had heard stories about people going to the other side. It was always a bright light at the end of a tunnel and an angelic being in a flowing white robe. There was no doubt after going to heaven that the first out-of-body experience was for real. I was not struggling with the reality of what had happened. I was struggling with how to describe what I experienced. This was my whale. Just like Jonah in the Old Testament, after breaking my neck and feeling that incredible evil, I should have shared it with the world. Jonah was given prophecy to take to Nineveh but he feared the same thing and he ran from God. Just like Jonah I did not feel that people would take me seriously and I spent the next twenty years running full speed from the same God who spared my life.

The next time I saw Dr. Kendrick while he was examining me, I asked, "Can you explain just what happened?"

Holding up my chart, he drew that same fist size circle and said, "I overlapped the edges and sewed the hole up."

Then he said very solemnly, "We scooped eight pints of clotted blood out of your abdominal cavity."

I reached for his hand and said, "Thank you for saving my life."

Dr. Kendrick replied, "You were dead."

He went on, "I did not bring you back, and I knew it was pointless to even give you the blood we gave you."

I knew now that he would believe me and I said, "I talked to an Angel."

Dr. Kendrick asked, "Did he send you back?"

Almost wishing I had stayed I told him, "It was my choice."

After a week in ICU they moved me into a private room and started to let me have solid food. Because of being late, I had not eaten anything on the morning of my accident, and in intensive care, they had only given me gelatin and broth. The room was small, and all that I could see from my window was the roof.

When they transferred me into the private room, they told me that some time that day someone from physical therapy would come up to work with me. No sooner than they were all out of my room and Gabe walked in and said, "What is it with you and twenty-five-mile-per-hour curves?"

I asked, "What do you mean?"

He explained, "You broke your neck on a twenty-five-mile-per-hour curve when you were in high school. Then you just tried to kill yourself of on another one of them. Both accidents were on Highway 11."

After Gabe left, my physical therapist came in. That first day she worked with me in bed, mostly stretching. Elizabeth was a small Hispanic woman and when she held my foot to her stomach and said push as hard as you can, I thought I would send her flying across the room. Her hands never moved and I could not believe that I was so weak. The incision to repair the lining slashed through my abdominal muscles like General William Tecumseh Sherman's slash-and-burn policy tore through Atlanta in the Civil War.

I was as weak as I had been in Galveston. Not at first but in recovering from a broken neck. This turned out to be a true ordeal for me. In the intensive care unit, I had actually wondered if death was still seeking my company. My stomach hurt so badly when I woke that I wondered if I was going to live.

Getting over this was going to involve going through a lot of pain. From my room overlooking the roof I had time to think about the things I had done wrong and the main thing that I did not do. I kept the channel changer on the television warm and my mind burning through heaven like a torpedo across a swimming pool. I could not take my mind off that big Angel or the way his eyes saw me.

This knocked me down hard; even my throat was in pain. The seat belt had crushed my larynx and to my great dismay they had performed another tracheotomy. I promise you, friend, that is something that you never want to have. To describe it, imagine drowning in your own saliva but there are a room full of nurses and doctors around you who are powerless to help you. A respiratory therapist will become your best friend after they cut into the trachea and insert a tube to force air into your lungs through. You will even long for them to visit to suction out the saliva that consumes you. When the suction tube enters the trachea there is always a sharp pain no matter how careful they are. The throat is a tender spot, and when that suction tube hits the walls of your trachea you imagine someone is cutting your throat with a butter knife.

After a week or so of working on sitting on the side of the bed and standing from the bed with a walker, I decided one night to try and make it into the bathroom on my own. To the right of my bed was the door to the hallway and then a mere twelve inches past the door was the wall. The door to the bathroom was at the foot of the bed, so in all it would be about a ten foot walk to my seemingly easy destination.

What made it so hard was the bathroom was to the left and to use the wall for support I had to use my paralyzed right arm to stabilize. I had some bicep from thousands of hours of curls, but to hold your arm out and steady yourself on something you are going to need triceps, and that I had very little of. If I held my elbow up with my hand on my chest, with fingers curled from paralysis, it felt like it was glued to my chest when I would try to swing it out. I had to hold the wall with my right hand and take steps to the side. Even this way it was not easy for soon those twenty-eight staples in my abdomen were on fire. Before even getting to the bathroom door, I knew that I was going to fall. I made it to the edge of the door and tried reached over and put my hand on the footboard of the bed. I heard the door swing open and Gabe said, "Boy, what are you doing?"

Knowing God had just saved me again I said, "I need help!"

To which my old friend replied, "After this boot kicks you in the seat of the pants." Then he said, "What were you trying to do?' Like a little boy with his hand caught in the cookie jar I said, "Going for a walk." To which my old friend retorted, "You are about to get the boot." With apparent anger in his voice Gabe asked, "Are you stupid?" After he sat me down on the bed I said, "Yes, Drill Sergeant." Gabe shook his head and in a pleading tone said, "Brother, I am not trying to be funny and this is not *Forrest Gump*." Then he asked me, "How many times do you have to die before you get it?" I looked up at him and said, "I will not give up." Relaxing a little he said, "Just be careful."

By the next week, Elizabeth would put a gate belt around me and we were walking in the hall using a walker. It was still so painful and I was so weak. All throughout the day and night I would lay there looking out the window at the roof working my legs. The hardest exercises were the abdominal exercises that Elizabeth had given me to do. Any amount of sustained movement caused me a great deal of abdominal pain and it would feel as though those twenty-eight staples were burning hot coals.

After another week, they transported me to Dallas to Health South hospital for my rehabilitation. I had some braces made over the years at this hospital and knew many of the people there. It was my only choice when it came time to choose a rehabilitation facility. It had formerly been Dallas Rehabilitation Institute, and my first stay there was to get my first full leg brace.

After fifteen years of walking in my partially paralyzed leg, it was hyperextending so bad the trainer at East Texas State University told me he thought it was going to break. Ed Sunderland referred me to a physical therapist he knew in Greenville and he sent me to Dallas.

The first person I saw when I walked into the building was a tall, beautiful blonde. She in turn saw me standing there looking just like a farm boy lost in the city and immediately walked over. She had all the charm of a southern belle but the sophistication of a princess when she said, "I am Ronnie Justice and you have the most beautiful eyes I have ever seen." I felt like I had just received an Academy Award and just like a farm boy lost in the city asked, "Where is the closest bathroom?" After the spinal cord injury when I felt the urge to urinate I did not have long and the urge had hit me when I pulled into the parking lot. There were three wheelchairs by the entrance that I supposed were used for guests, and this Greek Goddess in high heels quickly retrieved one and whisked me to the restroom.

That day I was only there for an evaluation, but Ronnie and her friends there got me approved for a thirty day stay to get a knee ankle orifice and gate training. My physical therapist was named Twyla and quickly became impressed with my work ethic. They made me use my manual wheelchair during the day and night to save my energy for physical therapy. That was a good thing because this building was huge and there was a lot to see. This hospital was on Harry Hines Boulevard which is notorious for strip clubs and street walkers. It just so happened that one of those strip clubs was right across the street and very conveniently there was an ADA compliant wheelchair ramp at the entrance. That means there was sixteen inches of slope for every one inch of rise. This ramp turned to the right as you rolled out of the door and stretched almost the length of the building. It was obvious to the eye that they dropped some serious bucks on putting in this ramp in anticipation of wheelchair caravans stopping traffic on a Dallas street to come to their club.

I ended up getting extra time to adjust to the new brace and relax in what was like a resort hotel to me. The man in charge of the cafeteria owned a five star restaurant in the Dallas area and was an award winning chef. Joel put a few pounds on my skinny frame. I managed to find a flower every day to bring to Ronnie whether it was from a patient's room or the crape myrtle tree out front. One night my cousin Rita was going to take me to this exhibit of this Egyptian king that was stopping in Dallas. Ronnie was a volunteer at the museum where the exhibit was and was going to be watching for us. That day I had found this little cheesy plastic flower somewhere and had taken it and put it on the door handle of Ronnie's car. That night when Rita and I saw her at the museum, I asked her if she found the flower I left for her. She proudly pointed to the neckline of her dress where she had the flower pinned and said, "I love it."

The brace made it so much easier to walk, but it was terribly uncomfortable and very hard to get on. It took a lot of effort and if I were going to wear my blue jeans I had to put them on simultaneously or they would take forever to get them over the foot plate of the brace. I would slide the right leg of my jeans through the brace and then put my foot through and fasten the strap around my ankle. There were hinges at the knee in the two metal bars made of titanium steel on either side of my brace. Above the knee there was a leather pad that wrapped around the thigh with two straps and buckles to hold it tight. Over the years they got smaller and lighter and much more comfortable. Dallas Rehabilitation Institute was now Health South and it had moved a few miles down the street closer to downtown. Most of the people were still the same and there was no question where I would go for rehabilitation.

Once again I was hit so hard doctors were telling me I would not walk again. I was worried about school because I was so close to graduating. It had been my dad's dream to see me graduate from college, and he was very disappointed when I dropped out. I had to do this for him, even now he would know. I was so weak and knew this could take a long time. So once again I settled in like a soldier in a fox hole waiting for the charge of the enemy.

My physical therapist was Kirsten Nelson, and she was one of the few bright spots in my long days. Kirsten and I were balancing sitting on this ball one day when I asked, "What is that?"

She said, "You mean the machine in the corner?"

Then I said, "It looks like a time machine."

Kirsten replied, "That is what it is."

Then she said, "You really are a college boy."

I asked her, "Why can't you just answer a question?"

The machine that I was referring to was called an Easy Stand Glider. It had a seat that you sat down on, and after you strapped in your legs, there was a leaver that you pumped to stand up. After you were in a standing position, it worked like cross-country skiing. With every free moment I had, I'd go into the physical gymnasium and get on the glider and workout. Toward the end of my stay there, Kirsten called the people who made the glider, and they sent a representative out to meet me. The company made one for me, and I went home with an eight-thousand-dollar workout machine.

One of my friends from Kilgore College called me almost every day of the nine weeks that I was in the hospital. Mike White went to high school with Cooter and back in the day had been a major party animal. As we were growing older, our partying was replaced by better choices and values.

One night on one of his phone calls, Mike said, "Scoot, when you get out of the hospital, come to Longview and live with me."

Wondering how I would make a living, I asked, "What am I going to do in Longview?"

Mike said, "You don't have to do anything. Until you are back on your feet again, you'll have a place to live."

After I got out of the hospital, I moved into the dorms to work on that last semester again. Someone had actually given Dr. Haung the rough draft of my paper, and she offered me a B for a final grade. I lived on campus because I no longer had a car and did not have a clue in the world what I would do to get one.

Albert Lopez's wife, Debbie, put together a benefit softball tournament to raise the money to buy me a new car. We had the tournament at Walker Park in Winnsboro, and even though there were only eighteen teams, there were hundreds of people there. Ricky Lopez even brought a team up from Fairfield where he lived. The one-day tournament lasted deep into the night, and people set up camps around the field.

I rolled up to the concession stand and asked, "Debbie, can I have a hot dog?"

Debbie said, "We're having a benefit. Do you have any money?"

She caught me by surprise, and being broke, I turned to leave. Debbie yelled, "Scooter, stop! This is all for you. You can have anything you want."

Smiling like a little kid, I asked, "Anything?"

Debbie asked Grocery Supply to donate the concessions, and there were hot dogs, Cokes, chips, and every kind of candy you could think of. As Debbie fixed me a hot dog, she said, "Look at all these people here for you, Scoot."

Looking around, I said, "Thank you so much."

She looked at me and said, "For what?"

I waved my hand at all of those cars parked around the outfield and said, "This."

With genuine sincerity, Debbie replied, "This was fun."

Looking fondly at my red-headed angel, I added, "But you have put so much work into this."

Then she told me, "Before I met you, all I heard was Scooter this and Scooter that."

I had to say, "I did this, but I did not do that."

Debbie smiled and said, "You are family, and we love you very much." Rolling her eyes like she were keeping a secrete, she said, "Do you want to know what we raised?"

Before I could say yes, she said, "We will finish with over eight thousand dollars"

Truly blown away, I exclaimed, "Wow!"

THE CALL

I graduated in the summer and by the day of the graduation had regained my strength and was ready to walk across the stage. Mrs. Eisenhower still worked for the University of Texas A&M University-Commerce and was there to make sure I had everything that I needed. When my group was called to the backstage area to prepare to walk, I got the jitters. I stepped out of line and said, "Y'all go on without me."

My friend who helped me get through algebra said, "Scooter, get back in line."

The girl behind her said, "If you don't walk, we all don't."

Another young man said, "You are going to hold up the whole show if you do not get back in line."

When my name was called and I walked across the stage, Dean Webber rose and made his way down from his perch where the dignitaries all sat with their pompous hats and met me. I was afraid he was coming to tell me that a last-minute check had determined that I was not eligible to graduate. When Colonel Webber got to me, he wrapped his arms around me and said, "I am so proud of you, Scooter."

Afterward people were coming up to me and telling me, "You are the only one any one got up for."

Mom told me, "Don't worry, I got a picture of it."

Gabe said, "Betty, it took him long enough."

Robert put his arm around my mom and said, "That's Ms. Betty."

Albert said, "You almost fell walking to the stage."

I looked at Mom and said, "Some lady sitting on the aisle flashed a camera right in my eyes."

Mom almost cried when she said, "I am so sorry."

After my undergraduate degree was completed, I had nowhere to go but graduate school. I could not teach because of my criminal background, and a bachelor degree in psychology is not worth the paper it is written on without a graduate degree. There was something more important than a master's or a PhD. I kept thinking about what that big angel meant: "There will be people who don't make it if you don't go back."

What people was he talking about, and where would they not make it to? Mike was still after me to come to Longview and stay with him. Mike was very active in his church and had let me know he could get in front of people to tell my story. I did not feel as though I had a story worth telling, and who would listen if I did?

Mike lived in a duplex on a dead-end street off of Gilmer Road. My friend Barry Eaves came up with Mike to help move me down to Longview. Mike already had furniture and with the exception of the things that were going in my room we put most of my things in storage. At the very end of the dead-end road was a water separator used by an oil company to take the water out of oil. The entrance that was used by this company to maintain this separator was at the end of another dead-end road. We were able to use that entrance as a driveway to our back door.

There was one step up on the front porch, and it was low enough that my Jazzy Power Chair would hop it. My bedroom was the back room and was where the back door was. There was about a three-inch drop from the bottom door plate to the patio. The bottom door plate with the storm strip made it difficult to hop in my chair. There were two-foot-long one-by-twelve boards on the patio, and Mike laid them on the door plate making a perfect ramp.

We had televisions in every room of the house and a giant Russian Blue cat named Elvis that was nearly as old as we were. I owed Texas A&M University-Commerce twelve hundred dollars to get my transcript released to potential employers. It may as well have been fifty thousand, and the job search for a disabled man without a degree was sad. Without my transcript, my degree was just a piece of paper in a pretty frame. Still I searched for a job with relentless determination.

One night, I was sitting in my room watching television when Mike came home and walked into my room. After tapping on my open door, he said, "Scoot, I got you a speaking engagement."

I asked, "Where?'

Mike told me, "I am putting together a men's crawfish boil at Woodland Hills Baptist Church. After everyone is served, I want you to speak for about twenty minutes."

Terrified, I asked, "Speak about what?"

Mike looked at me like I was an idiot and said, "The stuff you have been through is very inspiring. Many people are struggling with things not nearly as severe as what you have gone through and continue to deal with." Finally he said, "You inspire people, and you are a good speaker."

I replied, "I don't know about all that."

Mike cocked his head, pleading, "Do this for me."

Woodland Hills Baptist was on the loop and was easy for me to find. Mike had already been there for an hour or so preparing and boiling crawfish when I arrived. I had been asked before to say a few words at different events, but here for the first time I was going to be a keynote speaker. Long before I had gone to using a catheter, so peeing on me was the only thing I was not worried about.

After I was introduced, I slowly made my way to the podium with two hundred sets of eyes watching every slow move that I made. The applause stopped when I reached the podium, and I looked up and said, "Don't stop."

After I was through with my testimony, I was blown away at the show of emotion and support. A big man with a Gumby hairdo approached me and said, "Scooter, I am Steve Cochran."

He shook my left hand and said, "I was the pastor at First Baptist Winnsboro when you were terrorizing cows."

Smacking myself on the forehead, I said, "I thought you looked familiar."

Then he said, "I want you to come to my church this Wednesday night and speak to our youth."

Surprised, I said, "I would love to come!"

Almost immediately after that Wednesday-night service where over a dozen kids made salvation decisions, Cory Perkins, the youth pastor, asked me to come speak at the church's Bring-a-Friend Day. This would be a Sunday-morning service with up to two thousand people there. Because it wouldn't do to wear blue jeans and a T-shirt, Cooter took me shopping at the mall to buy a suit. I made seven hundred dollars for speaking thirty minutes, but it did not come close to paying for what we bought at Dillard's that day. It was an amazing morning, and Mike was there with me to help me up onto the stage and support me. There were salvation decisions and a line of people who wrapped around this enormous church waiting to meet and talk with me.

The only job options I had were in a call center providing customer service for Verizon Wireless. After a while, taking phone call after phone call took a toll on my voice. The call center noise level would get to the point that the people who were calling in thought we were having a party. By the end of my shift, my throat would hurt so badly from straining to be heard that it hurt to even talk.

One Saturday afternoon, I was driving to Winnsboro to visit the Lopez family and looked down and saw smoke coming from under the hood of my truck. My thermostat had stuck, and the truck had overheated really badly, and right away, I feared the block had cracked. Just by some miracle of God, I got a cell phone signal on this wooded country road and called for help. Cooter dropped what he was doing and came to help me, and a rancher who lived nearby offered his support. After checking my oil, fear that the block was cracked confirmed. They pushed my truck through a gate that I had stopped right in front of to wait for me to find someone who could put a new engine in it.

For several weeks, I took a cab to work and back home again. The managers at Sitel Corporation let me work all the overtime that I could to pay for my new motor. For those weeks, my work days were twelve and fourteen hours long. Then I would have to wait for a cab and sometimes have that cab drop me at Wal-Mart to get food. By the time another cab would pick me up and get me home, the midnight hour had come and gone.

This began to take an unbelievable toll on my health, but the main problem was with my voice. There were times that the people from the quality department would pull me off the phone and put me into training, because even they could not understand me. I worked in a small department that helped agents activate phones on the West Coast. Many of the agents who called our department would ask for me specifically; even though it may have been hard to understand me, the job performed was top-notch. It was not possible for another agent in the activation department to transfer a call to me, but agents would hang up and call back and call back.

One night, my phone beeped, and I said, "Thank you for calling Verizon Wireless Activations. This is Jimmy. How can I help you?"

A voice on the other end said, "Jimmy, you are the man! Only you can fix this."

Poking fun, I asked, "Do you mind telling me what you want?"

Daniel replied, "I held forever to get to you don't make me regret it."

Then I told him, "You Radio Shack people are like little kids. Don't be so sensitive."

Daniel got serious and asked, "Jimmy, can you help me out? I need you to speak to a customer?"

We were not supposed to speak to customers because we were strictly agent support, and there was an entire department devoted to customer support. Daniel knew that I would take time to figure the bill out and could calm his angry customer down before she deactivated four lines of service. She had called customer service and gone through wait time and multiple agents twice before and been disconnected. Looking at the bill, I could see how an agent might be prone to accidentally disconnect this call. I was just glad that my duties did not include messes like this one consistently.

In as fatherly of a tone as possible, I told Daniel, "Son, put her on the phone. Daddy is here."

A gruff voice on the other end said, "This is Betty Crumley. Are you the legendary Jimmy?" She went on to say, "Daniel said you can fix this."

In as soothing of a voice as possible, I said, "Mrs. Crumley, his confidence in me is well founded. Your international calling plan was outdated. The old plan was deleted, but in the update, the new code was not added."

Nearly every time I talked to someone for the first time, I had to explain that I was not sick. The reason that I talked the way I did was because I broke my neck in a car accident and had a paralyzed vocal cord. Expecting this lady who was angry with good reason to ask what was wrong with me or why this mistake were her problem, I heard her ask, "Jimmy, do you have a paralyzed vocal cord?"

That caught me so off guard, so I asked her, "How do you know that?

Then she told me, "My husband is a professor at University of California Irvine Medical School, and he just pioneered a surgery where they transplant a nerve into a paralyzed cord and make it work again."

Before I knew what I was saying, I said, "Oh my."

Then she said, "What are the chances?" Before I could say anything, she asked me, "What happened to you, Jimmy?"

I gave her the short version of my life story right there on the phone. She told me how interesting I was and that her husband would definitely want to help me. She gave me her home telephone and told me when I got off of work to call and talk to him. I added the code, for the international calling package created a case for the credits that needed to be applied. Before I let her go, I said, "This is amazing, Mrs. Crumley."

With a smile that I could hear, she said, "This is God, Jimmy."

After I released the call, turning my phone off, I stood up. My supervisor was a beautiful lady from Kenya named Queenie Olumbo. She saw me with tears in my eyes and from across the room asked, "All right, who made Jimmy cry? *Nakupenda*, Jimmy."

I said, "Nakupenda pia wewe dada yangu" (I love you too, my sister).

She told me that she loved me, and I told her that she was my sister and that I loved her too in Swahili. There were a dozen agents in the activation department that night, and everyone stopped to listen as I told them what had just happened. We were all very close, and everyone knew what a struggle it was on my voice to be on the phone for twelve hours. Everyone in the department was crying with me.

Queenie said, "Jimmy, go in my office and call him right now."

When Mrs. Crumley answered the phone, I said, "You sure got home fast."

She replied, "I am not home yet. The phones are forwarded. I talked to Dr. Crumley about you."

Excitedly I asked, "What did he say?"

Mrs. Crumley said, "He wants you to write him a letter and tell him all the things that you told me."

I thought that this was a nice way of blowing me off, but seven days after I mailed Dr. Crumley the letter, I had a return letter from him asking me to come to California for an examination. The pastor of Longview Metro Church paid for my airfare to Los Angeles. Rob Parsons was always helping me out, and we got an amazing deal with Air Tran. Because it was right across the street from the hospital, I got a three-hundred-dollar-a-night room at the Hilton. That was a lot of money for someone in my position, but I figured a small-town, crippled country boy would need the convenience and security of high-dollar accommodations.

After Dr. Crumley examined me, he told me that he could dramatically improve my voice and that he wanted me to come back for surgery in one month. From talking to a flight attendant on the way out, I knew Air Tran would fly me back for free.

After the procedure, Dr. Crumley did not want me to fly for a week, but there would be no reason to admit me to the hospital. The thing I worried about was coming up with two thousand bucks for a hotel room. For someone who grew up poor, spending that much money for staying somewhere for one week seemed ridiculous. The security and great location of the Doubletree made it the only hotel I considered.

The head of guest services at the Hilton was Diane Durniock. I went ahead and made a reservation for a week with her before I flew back to Dallas. My plans were to go home and work as much overtime as possible to pay for my week's stay at the Hilton. A few days before my flight back to Los Angeles, I called Diane to pay for the room. When she answered, I said, "Hey, Diane."

Right away she knew who it was and said, "Jimmy, are you excited?"

I said, "*Excited* is not the word for it."

Then she commented, "Everyone here is excited for you, and we can't wait for you to get back."

I told her, "I have the money saved to pay for my room."

Diane said, "We are taking care of that for you."

Surprised, I asked, "What?"

She said, "Your room is covered."

After the operation, the difference in my voice was like night and day. The only thing I had to pay for in my two trips to Los Angeles were souvenirs from Disneyland. There were so many cool people at that hotel. Being a simple man, when I see someone, I think how I can befriend them. I was not worried about what anyone thought of me, and even if I wanted, passing me off as a big shot in town on business would have been no fun. There were hotel employees who took their breaks in my room so we could talk. Diane took me out to lunch a couple of times and once had a limo take me to the pier in Santa Monica.

My first night on the phones after getting back from California, I took a call from Daniel. After I had given the official greeting, he said, "This is Daniel at Radio Shack. I've got a customer in my store that wants to see if she can get an early upgrade."

I was having fun with my friend because I knew that he had no idea who it was. I casually asked, "What is your customer's name?"

Daniel replied, "I'm sorry, sir. What is your name again?"

Thinking I was busted, I said, "Jimmy."

Plowing ahead, Daniel said, "Mr. Jimmy, my customer's name is Betty Sanchez."

Letting him off the hook, I said, "You never called me mister before. Are you scared, little boy?"

Angrily he asked, "What?"

In a pirate voice, I said, "This is Jimmy!"

He put the phone on speaker phone, looked at a coworker, and said, "Debbie, this is amazing." Then he told me, "Say something to Debbie."

From those early days in John Sealy hospital when I could not even scratch my nose when it itched, all I had ever wanted to be was independent. By this time, I was living by myself now— cooking my own meals and washing my own clothes. Every step that I took was a struggle, and every wall was my friend. It was an easy decision to walk a hundred extra yards if there was a wall to hold on to that would stop a fall. My routes for walks were planned to be near something that I could pull myself up on, in case of a fall.

A WRONG TURN

The hardest part of my day-to-day living was being alone in every single situation. Every night after I got off work and came home, it was me alone in a lonely house with my thoughts. Even when I was with my friends, it seemed to be that was loneliest time of all. Cooter lived only a short ten minutes away, even if both red lights caught you. Through Mike and Cooter, I had become an honorary member of Lake Cherokee South Side Social Club. There were so many friends who cared about me, but in the end, it was still the same, and I was all alone.

Working in call centers presented an enormous challenge for a person with a demonstrable disability like the one I had. If you are working in a call center with three hundred other people and can even get a handicapped parking place, there is still going to be a great many steps to walk in the course of your workday. Every day that I went to work there were people who had no disability at all who would take the best handicap spots. Many of them used placards they had obtained from a relative, and one guy even bragged to me about giving a kid a pack of cigarettes for one. One of the most frustrating thing things about my day would be the parking. There came a time when it got to me so badly that as a protest I refused to park in handicapped parking any more.

At Sitel Corporation, there were around thirty handicapped spots for just about three hundred employees. I was the only person there who walked with crutches. Mom's aunt gave her a power chair for me to use, and I left it at work charging just inside the conference room. The parking became such a sore spot with me that I started parking at the far edge of the parking lot and walking one hundred and fifty yards to the building. My thinking was that all those kids who were using someone else's handicap placard would see me and feel guilty and stop. My walking protest did not work out the way that I thought it would.

Years passed, and I was working in another call center, only this time it was an outsource for another phone carrier. One night on my last break, I was bumping the candy machine with my shoulder trying to make my cheese crackers fall when I heard the voices enter the vending area. Though I could not see them, I knew they were in the training class that had just started. This adorable little blonde who barely looked me in the eye with me sitting attacked the machine like she were blocking a blitzing linebacker and made my cheese crackers fall. She handed them to me and in a dainty voice said, "Here you go."

In shock at what I had just witnessed, I said, "Thanks."

She giggled and said, "Don't worry about it."

She smiled, and some man approached her and started talking to her, and my moment of opportunity was gone. The guy training her class was a friend whom I had known for a couple of years. Michael Chandler was way more country than me and was just a little less protective of me than Boseman had been. We had both abandoned Sitel for the better working conditions at Convergys at the same time. Michael was dating the most possessive woman on the site, so when I inquired about the cute, little blonde, he said, "I will hook you up!"

The next day I was in the McDonald's next door eating lunch, and she walked in and spotted me. After getting her order, she walked over to my table and asked, "Do you want some company?"

Before I could answer, she sat her tray on the table, and after she had taken her seat in her dainty voice, she said, "What's up?"

I looked across the table at her and asked, "How do you like your new job?"

She said, "Michael is a lot of fun. He talks about you a lot. He told us how you would bring all the plants in the building at Sitel to the activation department at Christmas and you guys called it Christmas in the Congo."

I said, "Michael runs his mouth a lot."

In the weeks that followed, Wendy and I began to talk more frequently and began texting secretly at work throughout the day. I had an operation on my right kidney and moved in to an assisted-living facility to recover. I continued to work, but with my chair being left at work the difficulty of everything else was amplified. After renting a place of my own one day Wendy and I were talking and she asked, "What are you doing tonight?"

I told her, "I have got to go back to my room and get my stuff packed. Barry is coming over to move for me."

Then she asked, "Do you need some help?"

I knew she had a boyfriend and had wanted to ask her out from the very beginning but did not think she would go. She ended up helping me pack that night, and I asked her for a date the next night. It turned out that she had just called off her engagement with her boyfriend but was dating her boss's son. She worked another job at night as a cleaning lady.

I was attending church at Longview Metro when I was not speaking at another church. An associate pastor there named Jerry Collom, who was like a father to me, gave me a word one day. Jerry was a giant, and because of his size and the way he took to me, I called him Big Daddy. In the mornings before work, I would go by the church and pray and usually spend time in Big Daddy's office. People in our church referred to Big Daddy as a prophet, and he told me that I was going to marry a beautiful woman with a grown child. Right after my big friend died, I met Wendy and she did have an eighteen-year-old son. Thinking she was the one Big Daddy spoke of, I foolishly plowed rocky ground.

Her son had two of his friends living with them in a two-bedroom apartment, and Wendy was working two jobs and still could not keep food in the house. The first time I came to her house for lunch, she had a plate for me wrapped in foil with tape on it that said Do Not Eat. She was working herself to death to provide everything that her son wanted. I wanted to hold this woman in my arms and never let her go.

On our first real date, I asked her son and his girlfriend if they wanted to go eat with us. We went to Pizza King, and I ordered a pizza for me and Wendy and a pizza for Taylor and his girlfriend. It had been a good idea, because we enjoyed our meal, and Taylor and I seemed to bond. After we finished our pizzas, we took them back to the apartment and went out and saw a movie. Wendy was the first lady who ever showed a real interest in me and definitely the first relationship to be physical. One night before we went to sleep, she told me, "I want you to wait six months to ask me to marry you."

My concerns with marrying her were that it appeared that everything that we ever did was going to revolve around her grown son. She was not concerned that her son and his live-in lover were having unprotected sex every day. She was actually looking forward to raising a grandchild and having a baby around the house. Totally convinced that Wendy was the lady Big Daddy spoke of in his prophecy to me, we married two months after our first date.

A week before we got married, I got fired for hanging up on the rudest customer that I had ever taken a call from. My throat was hurting from a cold, and the call center was very loud that day. This customer kept telling me that I sounded terrible and had no business being a customer service representative. Even after I explained what happened and that I was sick, she was demanding to be transferred to another agent. Even after trying to explain this to my belligerent, new friend that I could not transfer her to another agent, she called me a liar and demanded to speak with another agent. There was over a five-hundred-dollar bonus coming to me this month that was ticking away with each prolonged second of this call. When figuring commissions and bonuses, they looked for every way possible not to pay them to you. The number one goal in a call center is to handle the caller's issue the first time the call comes in as quickly as possible without transferring the call to another department. Your transfer rate and your call time are only two of the determining factor in receiving the commissions that you have earned.

There was no way to transfer her without her going back into the system and holding all over again, and much of the way your pay was determined was by your transfer rate, so I hung up on her. She had opted to take a survey at the end of the call, and when I released the call, it put her directly into the survey. She gave me the lowest score possible, prompting the quality department to listen to the call. Carolynn Garret was the call center operations manager, and I was called to her office. When I rolled into her office, she said, "Jimmy, pull up here beside me. We need to listen to a call."

Having a good idea what call it was, I asked, "Am I in trouble?"

She looked at me like the wicked witch from the *Wizard of Oz* and said, "You tell me."

After we listened to the call, she said, "So I can save your job, tell me that you did not hang up on her."

I asked, "Did you hear the way she talked to me?" Then not being one to lie, I said, "I hung up on her."

One night the first week after we got married, I was lying in bed watching television, and my stepson threw open the door and walked in. Not that big of a deal in hindsight, but then I was living with my new wife in an upstairs apartment because she had two bathrooms. I was just married and starting a job in another call center and was wondering if I could hold it all together. Though my duplex had two bedrooms, there was only one bathroom, and with three kids with us, that would not work. To say that I was stressed would have been a massive understatement. I had asked him to knock several times before and raised my voice when I said, "Knock on the door!"

My angry, little nemesis stepped back and slammed the door and exclaimed, "Crippled motherfucker!"

I waited to hear what my wife was going to say to him, but there was only the laughter of his friends. My first impulse was to get up and put my clothes on and get out and never come back. I was so in love with Wendy, and there had to have been a reason she did not defend me. I waited for Wendy to come to bed to find out why she did not say anything. When she finally came into the room, I asked, "Why did you not say anything to him?"

She gave me a puzzled look and asked, "What are you talking about?"

This was beyond belief, and I asked, "Are you serious?"

Again my precious, little wife said, "I don't know what you are talking about!"

At that moment, I realized what a terrible mistake I had made, and I said, "When your son called me that horrible name."

She said, "You should have seen the look that I gave him."

After that, she would hardly touch me, and her son referred to me that way often. Even if I did get her to kiss me, she would pucker her lips as if she were kissing me through a chicken-wire fence. I was coming home from work and then cleaning up the house and washing everyone's clothes in the hopes that maybe my new wife would spend some time with me when she got home. I thought maybe after she got through with her cleaning job, maybe she would come home and reward me with affection. Every day she got roses and little things like text messages telling her how beautiful she was. Nothing that I could do could bring the passion back.

We moved in to a duplex in Hallsville, and for a week, my stepson stayed in the apartment so he could be close to the restaurant where he worked. For a week, we were talking every night and watching television together, and every night we fell asleep in each other's arms in soft candlelight. Then after the lease at the apartment was up and my stepson moved in, things returned to the way they were. The apartment complex would not renew our lease because a string of cars that had been burglarized was traced back to my stepson and his friends. They tried to sell an expensive car stereo to the same person they stole it from. Every day I was at the office apologizing for something like screaming matches in the parking lot where my stepson's girlfriend called my wife a minimum-wage, crack whore.

There were five steps up to the landing where the steps to the second floor started. Taylor and his girlfriend were in the parking lot, and we were standing on the second-floor porch the night his girlfriend screamed, "You are a minimum-wage, crack whore!"

We had the police called on us nearly every day, and there was some kind of warning from the office regularly. I think my problem was that I was brought up in a different world. In the summer, I did more work in one week than her son had done in his life. My father worked me like a Hebrew slave when I was just a little boy. I could not wait to get away from home, and he did not want to leave.

I wish that I could have been a better man to my stepson, because he was just a kid. Maybe if we had got along, his mother would not have given up so soon. Wendy had promised to start going to church with me once we were married, but she only went one time. After we moved to Hallsville, I started going to Macedonia Baptist because it was so much closer, and I had watched so many of those kids grow up. Cory used me every time he had a big function with a lot of kids there. My precious wife came to church with me one time and then picked everything about the church apart. The reaction that Michael Chandler had when he found out what my stepson was calling me did not help me much either.

I did everything that I could do to help keep the house in good shape. It was getting harder for me to get around on foot, and I had applied for assistance to get a lift on my truck for my chair. If I could just get around better, I could do more around the house, and then maybe it would save my marriage. In an attempt to make things better between us, I added a line to my account so my stepson would have his own phone.

The phones were a major source of frustration, and I have a fifteen-hundred-dollar write off account with Verizon now. Wendy deleted every text message she got except for mine, and any time she sat her phone down near me, she would lock it. At night when she came home, she always let my stepson have her phone because his girlfriend had his. There were personal things about me that I said to my wife in text messages that he embarrassed me with. Nothing got better, and the whole thing with finding love and then losing it so quickly made me crazy.

Because I was not living the life I was called to lead, I did not help them. I was not in prayer, and I let my stepson, who was just a kid, make me act like a kid. After she stopped having a physical relationship with me, there were doubts that she stopped altogether. After we separated, one of her men friends told me that he had been taking care of my wife for me. Forgiving him would have been pointless, so I thanked him. Later on, I think Robert may have had a little talk with him about respect.

I had thought if there was more money coming in, then I could salvage what was left of my relationship with my wife. I began to look for a better job thinking that would fix everything. I interviewed with Aflac and was fortunate enough to get called back for a second interview. Dennis Caldwell offered me great hope that selling the security that Aflac offered their customers was my calling.

Mr. Caldwell said, "Jimmy, as soon as you have your license, I will put you to work."

Then I asked, "What do I need my license in?"

Mr. Caldwell said, "Life, health, HMO, long-term care, and annuities. When you pass the test, give me a call."

When I went to Prometric in Tyler to take my test, I had been studying for the test forty-five days. I kept telling Wendy it was going to get better, but she did not want to hear it. By the time I had my license and the lift for my chair on my truck and was ready to do better, all the love was gone. The day after getting my license, I called Mr. Caldwell to tell him I was ready. I gave two weeks' notice that morning, and Mr. Caldwell said to call him in two weeks, and he would put me with someone to train with. Every time I called him, he would put me off another week.

After I moved in with Wendy, I put all of my stuff in storage, and the pay of one hundred and nineteen dollars a month for that stressed things even more. By the time I realized that leaving was my best option, I had nothing to leave with. I lost the love of my life and everything else that I had accumulated over the years. I even lost the EasyStand Glider and my will to live.

I began to miss a lot of work because of issues with my kidney, and even with doctor's notes, the missed time counted against me. On top of losing everything else, I was in danger of losing my job now. The abyss of despair and depression that had enveloped me seemed to be insurmountable. With one bad decision, I had fallen out of God's will and lost everything that mattered to me.

My right kidney is partially paralyzed and does not drain as well as it should. Because of this urine, is constantly sitting in my kidney, and I began to develop kidney stones and be in and out of the hospital. When you go into a hospital for lithotripsy, you come out of the operating room feeling like you had been beaten in the ribs with a sledgehammer. I had so many operations in the Texas Regional Medical Center that I almost felt at home parking my truck in the parking garage and sleeping.

I went to physical therapy at AK Fitness and was able to shower there every day. My physical therapist there had been my friend since my first days in Longview. Leslie was at the Bring-a-Friend Day at Macedonia with her boyfriend. One day she was sitting at her desk talking to the gym owner. There were times when I would not be able to sleep because it were either to hot or too cold, and I would go to IHOP and drink coffee and then go to AK early. A few times, sleep depravity would overcome me, and I would park in front of the gym and go to sleep. When Joe got there to open up his business, I'd be asleep in my truck.

I pulled my chair up to her desk and said, "Good morning, guys."

Leslie said, "Hey, Jimmy."

Joe added, "Good morning."

I looked at Joe and asked, "When is the heat coming on?"

He replied, "It is warming up, but it is twenty degrees outside. It may take awhile."

Joe was just putting it together that I was sleeping in my truck, and I could tell it was really bothering him when he asked, "How do you stay warm?"

I looked at my therapist and said, "I think of Leslie."

She gave me a halfhearted smile and said, "Why don't you go to the mission when it is this cold."

I said, "I've been to the mission, and I am all right."

I was not all right though. I felt like I was trapped under that maintenance truck at Kilgore College, and my very soul was freezing. When I started seeing Wendy, I basically turned my back on all my friends. Wendy was not a social person, and she never wanted to be around any of my friends. After the things that I went through, they did not much care for her either. After all that time that I had ignored them, there was no way I could turn to them now—even though deep down it was easy to see that they wanted me to.

Things had been going along fine for me before I got married. I had some great friends who always included me in things. Cooter had introduced me to his CPA and good friend, who became my best friend. He was a graduate of Texas A&M and took me to Aggie games all the time. We were a real pair, he made thirty thousand a week, and I made minimum wage. When I met Perry, his girlfriend Rebecca was living with him. They had a stormy relationship, and when she packed up and left, I learned the most valuable lesson of all from watching Perry.

You can have a five-million-dollar home in town and a million-dollar home at the lake with a Corvette and a Hummer in the driveway, but that won't make you happy. Happiness is not as much connected to what we have as it is to what we give away. I knew that I was getting old, and there were not a lot of women looking for a crippled man working a minimum-wage job. So I made everything about hanging on to a woman who was in no way going to stay with me.

My favorite places to hang out during the days were at Books-A-Million and the library. I made some good friends there and read a lot of books without paying for them. Sometimes in the afternoon, I would pull my truck behind the store and park in a sunny spot and sleep. When it is really cold at night and you cannot afford to run the engine to warm up, you do not sleep much. When the Rangers were in the World Series, the only place I had to go watch it was at the Best Buy that was in the same shopping center as the bookstore.

When you are living in your vehicle, you come to find the safe places to park and sleep. You would think a parking lot at Wal-Mart would be a good safe place. People will walk by and knock on your window, and as they walk away, you hear them making fun of you. One Sunday, I was sitting in the café at the bookstore reading. These two ladies with a small child in a stroller sat down at table across from me and were sipping lattes and talking. I had not had a shower since Friday morning and had urine smell about me.

First, one of the ladies looked at me and said, "Do you smell him?"

The other lady said, "Let's move."

From the other side of the café, her child kept her eyes on me and had a big smile on her face. Her mother moved to the other side of the table. That little girl leaned way out of her stroller to just give me one last smile, and those two ladies got up and left. As they left the store, stoically I said, "You ladies have a nice day." Then I looked at the little girl and said, "Happy birthday!"

Her laughter exploded all over the building, and everyone watched as she waved good-bye with both arms as her mother ashamedly pushed her out of the store.

What happens from childhood to adulthood that would cause us to behave so differently? The little girl screaming when I said happy birthday was priceless. She was old enough to know that it was not her birthday, but she was young enough to know that we were having fun. People can't hurt you unless you let them, and exciting that little girl showed her mother that I had a heart.

STAYING ALIVE

If you see someone who is obviously down on his or her luck, then is the time that it is most important for you to reach out to them. Jesus did not tell Peter to pet his sheep. Jesus told Peter to feed his sheep. When you feed someone, you are giving them something that they need. When Jesus told Peter to feed his sheep, he was not referring to solid food. Human contact is a basic human need, and without it, emotional growth is thwarted. I never pass someone up who looks down. All that I can give them is a kind word, but that is what they really need the most.

Sometimes in order to sleep at night, I would take a couple of muscle relaxers. If I did not take pills to sleep, then I was sitting in Whataburger drinking nickel coffee and reading my Bible at three thirty. On the morning after taking pills, I might sleep until seven thirty. Those mornings I would wake up with hospital employees walking by my truck. Most of them were used to me, even though I only used the garage at the hospital if I thought it might rain.

There was an office that Wendy cleaned once a week that had covered parking behind it. It was not secure as the parking garage, but when they kicked me out of it, that was where I went in bad weather. They told me that if I came back, they would have me arrested for trespassing. The next time I had a kidney stone, I went to Good Shepherd Medical Center. To wake me up, they stood at the back of my truck and talked in loud voices. Then they practiced their Jerry Springer psychology on me. The security guard who talked to me sounded like he was country as a chicken coop.

He told me, "What we don't figure is why you are sporting this nice truck, but you don't have a home."

I said, "I have a home."

He asked, "Where do you live?"

I said, "It's right around the corner. If you'll move your squad car, I'll go there."

He looked at the golf cart behind me and said, "I am going to let you go with a warning."

Apologetically, I told him, "Thanks, Officer."

I backed my truck out of the parking space and headed out into the ice and snow to find a place to spend the night. The truly bad thing about this was even though it was freezing cold, I was sleeping like a baby. There was a truck stop out on the interstate that I went to sometimes to hang out that I could go to. They have rooms with showers that you can shower in for six dollars. These rooms have heaters on the ceiling, and you can turn them on and get the room very toasty.

The ice storm that had hit Longview had most of the city shut down, and it was a lonely ride on the loop to the interstate. There was not any rain falling, but there were snow flurries. I had borrowed a grill cover off a barbeque grill in Cooter's garage to cover my chair with. When your life becomes so dependent on an electric power chair, it is of major importance to protect it from the weather.

The best thing about the truck stop was that it was cheaper to eat at than my favorite night spot, but it was a long drive. When you had to watch your gas gauge like I did, every mile weighed into the equation. Since moving back to Longview, my favorite place to eat was IHOP. The owners knew me from my frequent visits, and we had become friends. One afternoon as I was leaving, the daytime manager followed me outside.

Joseph said, "Hey, Jimmy, let me talk to you for a minute."

My truck was parked on the side of the restaurant in front of the newspaper stands. I stopped and looked over my shoulder and said, "I did not do it."

Joseph smiled and said, "Jimmy, you are here so much we want to make you a VIP."

Thinking he would see the humor, I told him, "I'm a Baptist."

He smiled and put a piece of paper on top of the newspaper stand and began to write. Joseph asked, "Jimmy, what is your last name?"

I asked, "What does being a VIP mean?"

Joseph stopped writing and looked at me and said, "You get a 15 percent discount when you purchase anything at this restaurant or our Shreveport location."

Then I asked, "Do I get to fire people?"

He smiled and said, "Check with me first."

One night, the owner's daughter was introducing a new waiter to me. Nikki told him, "If Jimmy wants to substitute onion rings for hash browns, just do it."

Gabe shook my hand and said, "Jimmy, I have heard about you."

The draw to the truck stop was the shower room with the individual heater. I had on two sweatshirts with hoods and a small jacket but still had to run the engine to heat the truck. It would be cheaper, with gas over three dollars a gallon to get a shower room and sleep in my chair. I had taken a nap in one of them before sitting in my chair with my head laid on the vanity where the sink is.

The ice was thick where I parked, and as soon as I stepped out of my truck, my feet slipped out from under me, and I hit the ice with my butt first and then fell back. I was parked in a handicapped parking place in front of the door, and a truck driver saw me fall and came out to pick me up. He stayed with me to help me get my chair out and then get in the truck stop. My batteries were so low on my power chair, and there was a two-inch ledge where the inside door to the restaurant was. To get over it, the man had to go ahead of me and pick up on the front wheels and pull.

After thanking him, I slowly made my way to the store where the cash registers were to get a shower key. Then moving at a speed on inches per minute, with my towel and key, I headed to a shower room. After I unlocked the door, I turned on the heater and laid the towel out on the vanity. Then I plugged the charger on my chair in to the electric socket and went to sleep.

A knock on the door woke me up. I heard the cleaning lady say, "Are you all right?"

I answered, "Be out soon."

I had slept in the warmth of that shower room for three hours, and when I came out, the rising sun was casting beams of light through the breaks in the curtains. I had God to thank for getting me through another cold night. The eggs here, prepared any way you want them, were fifty cents apiece. I went into the restaurant and had coffee and ordered three hard-boiled eggs. The eggs could be eaten later; I had been living on peanut butter for so long they would be a treat. After the Aflac job never materialized, I got a disability benefit started, but it was just enough to make my truck payment. To keep gas in it was a continuous hustle because I never have or will beg.

I had three exceptionally close friends whom I turned to when I was in a serious bind. Of course, there was old childhood friend Cooter and the most faithful of all Mike, and then there was Barry Eaves. Barry was a brother to the end, and the fact that I had turned my back on everyone did not seem to bother him. I would not say that he understood why, because I am not really sure that I understand myself. I was going to schools and churches and talking to kids about the impact of their choices. Now I had to live with the consequences of my bad choices.

If I were going to go to church on Sunday morning, I either took a sink bath at IHOP or, if I could afford it, went out to the truck stop and took a shower. I became so ashamed that I started going to another church. I was ashamed of the way I had handled myself with my wife and her son. No matter what either one of them had done, I failed to reach them as a Christian man.

During those long, cold winter days, one of the places that I went to where I could stay warm was the Longview Mall. The first Saturday of each month, they would have a bluegrass music concert that was always a lot of fun. I was in the mall one day and looked at this big-biker sitting on a bench and did a double take. There was my old friend Danny Boseman sitting there. He was waiting for his wife, who had gone into Victoria's Secret. Danny knew through Ben that I was living on the street, and he took me to the food court and bought me lunch.

While we were eating, he asked me, "Why don't you let someone help you?"

I chewed my food and swallowed then said, "For so long I was so dependent on people for everything." After taking a drink of my Coke, I continued, "People fed me and wiped my butt for me. I got myself into this. I have got to get myself out of it."

I went to a prepaid account on my cell and actually was able to hustle enough to keep it on most of the time. I had an account with Metro PCS and had a cheap smartphone, but I could get on the Internet, and Facebook got me through many long nights. It was almost impossible to stay asleep when the temperature was in the twenties or in the teens. After suffering through a really cold night, I would spend a lot of time at the library. I'd go back to the back and sit at one of the back tables and put my head down and sleep. It was even harder to sleep if it were very hot. The only place safe enough to sleep with the windows down was the parking garage that had banished me to Tarsus.

I spent a lot of time at the library on the Internet applying for jobs. There was a rule that you could only be on the Internet thirty minutes at a time if there was someone waiting. They would give me extra time. but the lady in the genealogy department would let me use one of the computers in there all day if I wanted. She knew that I was on the Internet looking for a job and not just playing games or checking e-mail. I sent out so many résumés and applied for so many jobs every day that I knew something was going to come through.

I started doing some mystery shopping to earn some gas money. Staying clean was not a problem normally. I kept my dirty clothes in my locker at AK Fitness, and on Fridays I would load them in my truck and wash them that weekend. I kept a laundry basket in the floor on the passenger side with my clean clothes folded. I kept a toothbrush and toothpaste in my glove compartment, along with an ample supply of hand sanitizer and deodorant.

My urologist worried about me a lot. Every time that I went in for an office visit, he would tell me, "Jimmy, if you need anything, will you call me?"

I would always say, "Yes, Dr. White."

One day, he told me, "Jimmy, you need to start using an internal catheter. Your right kidney is not draining properly. You keep fighting me on this, and you will lose your right kidney." Next, he drew a simple outline of a kidney and pointed to the frontal lobe and said, "This whole portion of your right kidney has crystalized."

They either put me to sleep and let an elephant stand on my ribs, or they broke up the crystallization with lithotripsy.

After he finally talked me into letting him insert a catheter into me, it actually made life better. In the first place, I was not sick all the time, and then it just made life easier. After the catheter was in, you do actually forget it. Wendy was long gone with other men and had told me sex with me did not do anything for her anyway. She made me feel as low as worm, and even after she said things like that, I tried to win her back.

I forget how Melanie and I got back in touch with each other. She was my classmate and friend from growing up. I had worked for both of her parents at one time or another and had been in and out of her house all my life. Melanie had married Joey Windham, and they had just bought the Chevrolet Dealership in Quitman. Before I met Wendy, I bought a brand-new regular cab, Silverado. Without that truck, my life would not have been worth a plug nickel. The only reason that I still had possession of my truck was because one of my dearest friends was the president of the bank that held the note.

ANGEL ON MY SHOULDER

Having a friend like Jan had saved me on many occasions. If you ever go through a hard time and one of your oldest and best friends is a bank president, it will help. Sandra had been her assistant for a long time when she retired. She was like a mother to me, and when she left, I had my doubts that the blonde taking her place could ever fill her shoes. Julie Huffman turned out to be one of the most dependable people I had in my life.

One cold night, I was moving to find a place more protective from the wind when my phone rang. It was ten o'clock at night, and it was fourteen degrees. There were no other cars on the deserted stretch of road that I was on, so when my phone rang, I pulled over. It surprised me to hear Mom say, "Are you all right?"

Immediately I asked, "What are you doing up so late?"

Mom's desperation was apparent when she said, "Do you have a place to spend the night?"

Then she said, "I have been watching the weather, and it's going to get down to ten degrees."

Trying to put her at ease, I told her, "I am on my way to Mike's."

Before she said anything, I heard what sounded like a small dog yelping under the hood of my truck. Then the yelping stopped, and there was a clicking noise that lasted for a few seconds before I dropped my phone and turned the engine off. Usually when you kill the engine, the lights stay on momentarily, and the dome light comes on.

However, this time the lights went off immediately, and the dome light did not come on. Fear shot through me like an electric current through new copper wire. I tried to start the truck, and not even the red check engine light would come on. I reached up and hit the OnStar button, but nothing either. My truck had gone from driving down the road to no power and a dead battery in an instant. I reached for my cell phone, but it was not where I thought I had dropped it.

This was the coldest darkest night I have ever seen in my life. I could not see my hand in front of my face, much less have seen where that small black phone was adeptly hiding. Desperately feeling under the console and under the seat for my phone only turned up a phone charger that had been lost long before.

As cold as it was, there was no way I could get out of my truck. It was really hard for me to move in severe, cold weather. Even if I got my chair unloaded, there was not enough juice in my batteries to get anywhere. The only thing I could do was try and keep warm until daylight and find the phone and call for help. At least inside this icebox with four wheels, I was out of the wind.

The first hour was as miserable as anyone could be. This was the coldest I had ever been, and even though I was tired enough to sleep easily, like the day under the maintenance truck knew better. I flipped the console up and stretched out in the seat of the truck and began to think that maybe I should just go to sleep and take my chances. Things were not going too well for me, and I had gone back before, leaving the presence of God for this. There were several hundred people whose lives had been touched and changed after hearing my testimony. Maybe he was through with me.

This was indescribable pain as my limbs froze, and my organs shut down my life began to fade to black. Shaking profusely from the cold, I was thinking back on the times that death had been so close before, but somehow God had pulled me though. Then turning onto my side, facing the glove compartment, my thoughts drifted. There was a box of lemon drops in the basket with my clean clothes, and I thought sucking on hard candy might help keep my mind off the cold. Feeling around in the basket, my hand brushed against something small and dense. I felt around the spot, and there it was; I had found my phone.

Praying that it had enough charge to make a call, I went into the phone book and started looking for the eight hundred phone number to OnStar. My one-year free subscription that came with the truck was long since expired, but they had helped me before, and this was an emergency. The number was not in the phone, and I had to swallow my pride and ask for help. The first person I tried to reach was Cooter. Then I tried Barry and went through my Longview friends like a hot knife through butter. No one answered their phone at three thirty in the morning.

According to the weather on my phone, the temperature was an icy ten degrees a mere twenty-two degrees below freezing. I saw Julie's name and thought, *Well, it is worth a try.* Julie Huffman answered the phone on the second ring and asked, "What is wrong?"

I said, "I am so sorry to wake you up."

She asked again, "What is wrong?"

I said, "Julie, I am broke down and freezing cold. I need you to look up the phone number to OnStar for me?"

Julie got me the number, and I told her exactly where I was. She offered to call one of her friends in Longview to come and get me. My truck was my home and had become the only security that I had, and I had to stay with it. I assured her that everything would be all right, and we hung up.

Thinking that my truck would more than likely be towed, I was wondering what I was going to do and where would I go. Long before my urologist talked me into going to an internal catheter, I started using an external catheter, also called a condom catheter they roll down the genitals and are self-adhering with a connection on the end that connects to a hose attaches to a bag on your leg. I checked my catheter, and thinking that OnStar would tow me, I thought I had better change it.

I reached in the glove compartment and got a catheter and found a box of baby wipes to clean myself up. This was on a Saturday night, and I had not taken a shower that morning. I had on a pair of nylon sports pants and slipped them down to my knees so I could get started. The moment I got my pants down, a sheriff's car pulled up beside me. The deputy got out of his car and approached me with a flashlight shining in my face. Unable to lower my window because of the electrical problem, I opened the door just a little.

The deputy said, "We got a call that you were in trouble."

Then he tried to open my door, but I held on to it. In apparent anger, he said, "Let go of the door!"

I let the door go, and he opened it and said, "You are going to jail! I hate catching some pervert jacking off."

I held the catheter up and told him, "Officer, I have a medical condition and have to wear this."

The second that she hung up with me, Julie called the sheriff's department to get them to come and check on me. The deputy apologized profusely and hooked his battery cables to my truck, and it started right up. I went to Whataburger to drink coffee and thought about this. Why did my truck lose power while the engine was running? Was this the hand of God diverting me from some unseen disaster?

My one place to go where I really felt at home and could relax was McCann Street Cigars. The owner was a huge man and covered with tattoos. Jimmy owned a tattoo parlor on the other end of the building. Sandwiched between the cigar sop and the tattoo parlor was Barry's dental lab. Years before, Jimmy had given me an autographed portrait of John Wayne that had been hanging on the wall in the cigar shop. I was always admiring it, and one day I was sitting at a table smoking a cigar with Jimmy, and his wife sat the beautifully framed picture on the table in front of me. Jimmy said, "Scoot, we love you and want you to have this."

Jimmy gave me that picture before I got married, and it is the only thing that I still have. It never went into storage with the rest of my things because I knew there was the possibility that I could lose everything. Jimmy is a hard man who has done hard time, and I never took his gesture of remarkable kindness lightly. Many times, he let me use the bathroom in the cigar shop to clean up, and a few times, I left my chair there overnight to charge.

There is a massive cemetery across from the tattoo shop, and I would cut through it on my way to Kroger's to buy peanut butter. Once I was all into looking at these old markers, and I got stuck so bad that even when I stood up, I could not drive my chair out. The operators in the emergency call center knew me to the point they would tell other operators they had me on the phone. This operator dispatched an officer in a patrol car to help me. I saw the patrol car pulling up behind me, and when the door opened, I heard the officer say, "This is first for me."

Once before I was married, my chair got stuck, and I called Jimmy's brother John, and he showed up in a four-wheel drive Expedition with an eighteen-inch lift kit on it. His truck was so high I could duck and drive my chair under it. It was the day after a good rain, and I went to pick up a drink can that had been thrown out in my yard and got stuck. John pulled up, and he got out of his truck taking pictures of me. Before he pushed me out, he said, "This is going on YouTube."

One time during the height of winter, Cory talked Pastor Cochran into letting me stay in the vacant parsonage for the children's pastor. This house was a nice brick home that was within view of the church. Macedonia Baptist has a campus on an oil-top road a few miles off the loop in Longview.

They could only give me two weeks there because they could not give that option to everyone in the congregation who was down on their luck. One of the things that they asked of me was for me not to draw attention of my presence there. If at all possible, I was to stay in town during the day and come there only at night to sleep. One particular day, it was sleeting and snowing, and I had been dreading leaving the bookstore all day. My friend there who was the barista at Joe Mugs Coffee kept me supplied with coffee on those cold days. Books-A-Million closed at nine o'clock, and I had to head out into the snow and ice and head out of town to the children's parsonage.

The batteries on my power chair were very low because I had been zooming around the store all day. I knew there would be enough charge in them to get inside the house and charge them while I slept. There was not a bed in the vacant parsonage so I slept in a recliner in the master bedroom. The only key that I had to this really nice house was to the front door. After pulling my truck into the driveway and unloading my chair a sidewalk led up a slight hill to the front door. My low batteries completely gave out less than halfway up that hill.

The snow and sleet were coming down pretty hard and there was only one thing left for me to do. I had an inverter in my truck that plugged into my cigarette lighter and had an electrical plug that I could plug my chair into to charge. Getting back to my truck should be easy because it was downhill, so carefully I started to turn around.

As careful as I was and as slowly as I were moving the back wheels of my power chair slipped of the icy sidewalk and into the snow on the frozen ground below. It was only a drop of three or four inches at the most, but with my batteries as low as they were I was stuck like super glue. The house was far enough off of the road and there were enough trees in the front yard that even if someone drove down that lonely oil top road, they would not see me.

My cell phone was in my pocket and I never hesitated on what to do. I had called 911 so many times before that the operators in that area knew me. The rescue personnel that came were actually from Hallsville because I was just outside of Gregg County. It seemed like hours that I sat there in the sleet and snow waiting on the recue vehicle to arrive. One of the EMT's tried to hide her tears after they had pushed me into the house. They pushed me back to the master bedroom and helped me get into the recliner and then plugged my chair in to charge.

Another time I was sleeping in my truck in the parking garage at Regional Hospital and somehow managed to roll off onto the floor. There was absolutely no way that I was going to wiggle out of this one and pulled my phone and dialed 911 for help. A patrolman and a fire rescue truck came to get me out of this one.

LONG ARM OF THE LAW

I knew several Longview Police Officers and believe me that worked to my advantage more than once. One of the nicest fairest Law Enforcement Officers that wears a badge in the great state of Texas is Sargent David Scott. It really was my good fortune to meet him in Books-A-Million in the café.

I was studying for my insurance exam at the bookstore, and I see this man sitting at a small table with two small children and a textbook the size of a Pharisee Bible. He was taking a graduate class in philosophy and undoubtedly was an intelligent man. I have a better-than-average knowledge of the ancient Greek philosophers, so I struck up a conversation.

It turned out this ordinary, back-to-school dad is a sergeant on the Longview Police Department and was working on his PhD. After Sergeant Scott's graduation, his fellow officers dubbed him Dr. Sergeant Scott. He was a bright spot in my days, and I think that he was just checking on me some of the times when he came in. Knowing him sure worked to my advantage one night.

One afternoon, I went into Hastings to read and relax and get out of a two-day deluge of rain. I had been reading the book *Pinheads and Patriots* by Bill O'Reilly. I would mark my place and then stash the book somewhere where no one would find it. When I went back in, I would go get the book and take up where I left off. I finished the book that night but found it still to be pouring down rain when I was ready to leave. Hastings was closing, and I had to go outside. The bookstore I had been in was in a shopping center with Albertsons and another book and gift stored called Barron's. There were little stores like a Game Stop and a Hallmark shop.

Down the sidewalk was Baron's, and there was a patio area where I could try and wait out the rain. The night air was cold and drove a hurting chill down into my bones. The wet ground cooled things down even more. As a homeless quadriplegic, the weather and its many moods had become my worst enemy. There was no telling how long this rain was going to last. I sat there for a few more minutes then went down to Albertsons to get out of the cold, wet air.

The rain showed no sign of letting up, and as I was sitting there in front of the door waiting for the rain to stop, a young man who worked there walked up and asked, "Do you need some help getting your chair in your truck?"

Feeling like I had just been rescued by the Calvary, I replied, "You are a lifesaver. The hard part is getting the cover on my chair after it is on the back of my truck."

He then asked, "What do you need me to do?"

Tenderly I asked, "Will you get in the back of my truck and put the cover on when I get the chair loaded?"

The young, energetic young man said, "Let's go."

Just like that after all that waiting, I headed out in to the pouring rain to get my chair loaded. When I did this by myself, the cover went on the chair before the chair went in the truck. I would use the lift to swing the chair all the way over behind the passenger side of the cab to get it out of the wind and protect it from the rain some. Just before I lowered the chair all the way down, I would walk around the truck and make sure the cover was tucked under the wheels so it would not blow off.

I would have been soaked if I had done this on my own, and after we got it in, I told him, "You just saved me."

He replied, "I see you all the time. Anytime you need help, just find me."

I got in my truck and watched him walk away. He was just about the same age as my stepson, and I felt a pain in my heart for the way that I things had gone between us. There is a bank at the southwest corner of the loop and McCann Road, and I pulled up underneath the drive-through to protect my chair and wait. I parked in the lane next to the ATM machine and started reading a book about the war in Afghanistan. If I had not have had that accident and the famous cookout had never taken place, I'd probably be there right now.

After an hour or so of reading, I grew sleepy, and the good thing about living in your truck is that your bed goes with you everywhere you go. It was getting late, and I thought that I may as well wait out the rain napping; I flipped the console up and lay over to sleep for a while. I woke up to the rapping noise of a flashlight hammering away on the driver's-side window.

I opened my eyes and saw this massive police officer with a crew cut screaming at me in a German accent. He yelled, "You in the truck, step outside."

I rose up and turned the key on and lowered the widow, and he asked, "What are you doing?"

Trying not to sound facetious, I replied, "Sleeping."

The big police officer said, "This lane is for banking, not for sleeping."

I looked at the closed bank and said, "Yes, sir."

Then he said, "Give me your driver's license and insurance."

This man was so gung ho that before I made a move, I asked, "They are in the glove compartment. Can I reach for them?"

The officer looked at my eyes and said, "Why are your eyes so red?"

Pleadingly I said, "I have been sleeping. I pulled under here to wait out the rain."

Then he said, "I will be right back."

He turned to go back to his patrol car and stopped and asked, "What is your address?"

I replied, "I don't have one."

Then he asked, "Where do you live?"

Looking at the clothes basket in the passenger floorboard, I told him, "In this truck."

The impact of what I said hit him hard as emotion showed in his eyes, and when I opened the glove compartment, he saw a bottle of pain pills. He got in his patrol car and proceeded to count the pills in the bottle. Another officer had arrived by then and told me they were waiting on their sergeant. The big German came back and said, "We are arranging transportation to take you to jail."

Almost in tears, I asked, "Why am I going to jail?"

At that moment, another patrol car pulled up, and the big German said, "My sergeant is here, and we are going to get you off the streets."

I thought maybe he was just trying to be a Good Samaritan and get me a place to sleep. How could he possibly think that putting me in jail could be better for me? I could hear him talking to his commanding officer in a low voice, but then his sergeant raised his voice, and I figured out who it was.

Dr. Sergeant Scott told him, "Let him go!"

The officer came back and said, "Sir, I was trying to get you out of this weather. Here is my card with my cell number. Any time you need help, please call me."

Being homeless has got to be hard for anyone, but for a man with paralysis in a large portion of his body, it was taking a huge toll on my physical and emotional health. There were no outside forces to blame for my circumstances or for my diminished physical condition. With every bad choice that I had made, it set forth a set of consequences that I had to endure and suffer through.

Sometimes our suffering may be brought on by disobedience, and other times, God may use it to refine and shape us. My disobedience had definitely brought on my suffering, but at the same time, it was developing my character. With every sleepless night in my truck, there was time to reflect and pray. Many nights I would park in front of the well-lighted Burlington Coat Factory to study my Bible. My favorite book to study was the book of Job.

While there were truths found in the accusations of Job's accusers, they did not apply to Job. On the other hand, each and every setback and pitfall that befell me was due to my bad choices. Still, there was solace to be found in the recovery that Job made after the devil was through attacking him.

Believe it or not, the summer was a lot worse than the winter. Sleeping in my truck was frightening because I worried about being victimized by crime. There were times when the sound of footsteps walking around my truck woke me. I could not leave my windows down far enough for someone to get their hand inside, and that made for some long, hot nights. Many times during the night, I did not sleep at all and waited for the security of daylight to sleep.

Once on a visit to Dr. White, he asked me, "Jimmy, how are you holding up to this heat?"

I told him, "It is not that bad."

Then he said, "You have bacteria in your bladder that is best treated with intravenous fluids."

Going on, he said, "This is a bad infection. Why don't you let me put you in the hospital?"

Shaking my head, I said, "Then I am right back on the street again."

He said, "Stay in the hospital for three days, and then we'll get you into a nursing facility for thirty days."

With a ray of hope lighting my heart, I asked, "You can get me in a nursing home for thirty days?"

My doctor told me, "Medicare will not pay for a nursing home until you have been in the hospital for three days. We can get you admitted right now." He winked at me and asked, "Are you packed?"

I told him, "I love you."

He said, "I love you too, Jimmy."

The nursing home was a great break, but in my hospital stay, I missed an interview at Books-A-Million. I called and explained my situation to the general manager. Ty, who had only been at the Longview location for a few days, did not know me like the rest of the staff. He told me, "Jimmy, I have to think about my employees who would have to cover for you every time your doctor puts you in the hospital."

In desperation, I said, "This will never happen again."

Ty said, "Call me when you get out, and we will set something else up."

Gratefully I said, "You will not regret this. I will work so hard."

Ty said, "Jimmy, you don't have a job yet. I just said call me."

After my thirty-day vacation from sleeping in ninety-degree heat, I finally landed a job at Books-A-Milion. My hours were very limited, and I was lucky if I got to work one day a week. All of the employees there were young, and with the exception on Price and Kerrie, they were high school kids working for spending money. I put up sale books and helped put books that had been moved back in their proper place.

I worked hard and was always asking Ty for more time. There were eighteen-year-old kids who were working forty hours every week who did not give nearly the effort that I did. There was an eight inch-step up to the platform where the cash registers were, and in my wheelchair, I could not get behind the registers. The way it was explained to me was that my hours could not be increased because I could not relieve the people working the cash registers on their break.

One afternoon, I was sitting in my truck reading a book called *The Horse Soldiers*. A good thing about working at the bookstore was that I could check out as many books as I could read. I read so many books about the fighting in Afghanistan and Iraq it seemed as though I had been there. The book *The Horse Soldiers* was about special forces soldiers who commandeered horses and rode into the first major battle in Afghanistan on horseback.

Sitting there in the shade with both windows down, the autumn air felt good. My phone rang, and the display showed Aflac. I was thinking, *Well, maybe Mr. Caldwell is just getting around to calling.* I answered, "Yeah."

A voice on the other end said, "May I please speak to Jimmy Drew?"

Realizing this was not the man that I thought it was, I said, "Yes, miss, this is Jimmy."

She said, "Jimmy, my name is Rebecca, and I am with Aflac."

A lady called me trying to get me to come into the Tyler office for an interview. I thought that maybe the timing just had not been right the first time, and this was my big break. We sat up the interview for one o'clock the next day. That night, I sat in IHOP drinking coffee and reading everything Mr. Caldwell had given me on Aflac the first time I went through this process.

A good place to sleep in a safe area was beside Luby's Cafeteria. Luby's back door faced IHOP's backdoor, and the only thing between them was fence and some dumpsters. The parking lot on the east side had a tree that I could pull my truck under in case of rain. IHOP was open all night, so on the weekends, it got very loud.

This place was so close to AK Fitness that I did not even have to get on a street to get there. I had my shower and thought that I may as well head to Tyler and hang out. I got on the loop to head around Longview, and I saw the building that the Longview office is in. This was something that I should have done a long time ago, but I pulled into the parking lot of the Austin Bank building to find out why Mr. Caldwell left me hanging.

When I rolled into the Longview Aflac Regional office, I saw two men sitting in an office to my right talking. They greeted me, and I went inside to talk to them. They introduced themselves, and then I told them my story. When I left there that morning, I was working for the Longview regional office. One of the men told me that he had actively been seeking a person with a disability to work for him and that I was going to make so much money. The only money that I ever made was on a policy that I sold myself, and to make it worse, I left the bookstore for greener pastures. No one ever took the time with me personally to show me the ropes. Oh, I was given a few pamphlets to read but then was thrown to the wolves.

Coming into Aflac, I was going to do cold calling and set appointments for other agents and do a sixty-forty commission split. I set a lot of appointments, but they never closed any groups or made sales. There was really only one agent who would even let me know what happened on the appointments. Rob told me one day, "The appointment in Gladewater will be a hundred-man group, and you will make in the thousands."

Every couple of days, he would tell me what was going on and that we were going to get it.

My boss told me one day, "If we don't get some money in your pocket soon, you will be gone."

Now on top of everything else, I was going to get fired. I asked, "You are going to fire me?"

Mr. Phil said, "Jimmy, you cannot keep working your butt off for free."

Then I said, "I need to be able to run my own appointments, because there are agents who will blow them off and then call me to reset them."

My boss just said, "We need to get you trained on that."

Most days, I sat around waiting for someone to take me on an appointment with them. The only time management ever offered training to me was when I could not get my chair out of my truck because of my lift was broken.

Right before I left the bookstore, Ty had given me a fifty-cent-an-hour raise and a title. Not any more hours, but it was three dollars more a week and a title. With the promise of riches, I sent a text to a friend and said that I wasn't coming back in. That was just like writing it in spray paint on the wall in front of the store. Without a ramp to the cash registers, I would never go anywhere, and they did not want to put one in. I could get it put in, and Ty said he may be able to get the store to pay for the material.

It was not much, but I wished to God I had stayed at the bookstore. I asked about giving notice, but my new boss told me he could only give me a job right now. I could not look Ty in the eye and tell him I was quitting without notice. I set myself up to fail in Aflac because of the way that I left the bookstore.

FADED MEMORIES

One weekend, I drove the hour and half of twisting country highway to Sulphur Springs to see Gabe and Carla. Carla would always do some laundry for me, and Gabe was a grill master. Their oldest son had just graduated from Texas A&M in College Station, and this would be the first time I had seen Mitchell since he walked across the stage. He had been there at my graduation yelling his young head off. Their younger son, Tanner, still had a year of high school and was having trouble finding a college with a degree program in skateboarding or sleeping. I had been picking on him since he was a little boy and asked Carla to wake him when I got there. One in the afternoon was the cutoff time for breakfast at the Cordova estate anyway.

When I got to Gabe and Carla's house Friday afternoon, no one else had arrived yet. There were going to several people coming in that weekend for a crawfish boil. The one I was most excited about seeing was Robert. Once Gabe and Robert had taken me to a club in Yantis, Texas, called East Fork. They called it that because it was on the east fork of Lake Fork. I had just got out of the hospital from the second bad accident, and a night of winding down with two old friends was just what I needed.

When we got there, they got my chair out of the back of Robert's truck and then got me into it. I had just got a new power wheelchair but never got to use it anywhere but around the house.

We got inside the club, and Robert said, "Gabe, you and Scooter go to the back and get us a pool table. I will go get three beers."

I said, "Robert, I am drinking liquid hydrocodone for pain. I can't drink beer."

Gabe looked at Robert and asked, "Tequila?"

Robert replied, "Better make it two."

On our way to the back, Gabe was in front of me running interference when this local yahoo told us, "You and your crippled pet go around me."

When Robert got to the back, he saw Gabe up in the guy's face, and he went into protective mode. Charles had been murdered by three punks in a robbery nine years before, and at the funeral, he told me, "You are the only brother I have left."

I said, "Robert, you have brothers who love you."

He said, "You and Chuck raised me."

I had to do something quick, or Robert was about to literally kill this man. Gabe looked at Robert and said, "This gentleman just called Scooter my crippled pet."

Robert dropped the drinks and lunged at the man, grabbing him by the throat with both hands. It took a dozen of our friends to pull Robert off this man, but still, he got up and said, "If you have the nerve, we can go outside and dance!"

Even now, this was a game to him; he did not see the fury in Robert's eyes. He had no idea of the ferocity that would be unleashed on him if he fought Robert.

When we got outside, Gabe asked Robert, "Please don't do this."

I was talking to the man who had called me a crippled pet. I said, "Buddy, you are making a huge mistake."

He said, "I am sorry for what I said about you, but I am kicking his butt!"

He finally saw the seriousness in my eyes when I told him, "Our other brother was murdered, and he could not stop it." Pleading with him, I said, "He will kill you."

Somebody whom I did not know approached him and whispered something in his ear. They walked away, and Gabe said, "I got beer at the house."

Going to Gabe and Carla's for the weekend was always a treat with great home cooking and a big bed to sleep in. The last thing that I was going to do was be a burden or a bum to any of my friends. I did not feel embarrassed around Gabe and his family. I was ashamed of myself for living in my truck and eating peanut butter for breakfast, lunch, and dinner.

Monday morning when Gabe and Carla left for work, I headed back to Longview. I went by McDonald's to get a Sausage Biscuit before I hit Highway 11 and headed to Winnsboro. Leaving out of McDonald's, I looked in my rear-view mirror and saw a highway patrolman with his lights on. I pulled over and watched the young officer get out of his patrol car and approach the passenger side of my truck with his hand on his gun.

As he approached, I was thinking, *If I don't get shot, I will get three tickets. I will get one for whatever he is stopping me for and both my tags and my inspection sticker were out.* By the time the officer got to my truck, the window was lowered, and he asked, "Can I see your license and insurance please?"

This police officer scared me because as I sat there with both hands on the steering wheel and a power wheelchair in the back and handicapped plates, he still had his hand on his gun. Politely I said, "They are both in the glove compartment, and it is unlocked."

He asked me, "Did you know you were doing forty-five in a thirty-five?"

I replied, "I thought I was in a forty-five."

He carefully extracted them from the glove compartment and opened up his ticket book. Thinking anything was worth a try, I said, "Officer, I have been homeless for a year. I don't have job and only have insurance because of my stepdad." Finally, I pleaded, "Please don't give me a ticket."

His reply was, "Do you know your registration is out?"

I said, "Yes, sir."

The policeman said, "You will be receiving a citation for that as well."

I did not always survive on a jar of Peter Pan. With just two dollars, I could go to Taco Casa and have two bean burritos with cheese, onions, and lettuce. They had a television that I could watch the news on and relax. Most of the time when I ate there, I went through the drive-through and parked in the parking lot.

Once I was sitting in the parking lot eating a burrito and drinking a cup of water, Cooter and Freddy's wives walked out. I lowered my head and hoped they would not see me. Freddy was Cooter's cousin and had been around a block or two with us.

Freddy was mentally and physically harder on me than anyone that I knew. At times, Freddy made me want to shoot him in the head with a Trident nuclear missile. He would do anything in the world that I asked of him, except for lay off of me.

Cooter and Dawn live in a house on a cul-de-sac, and one night there were a bunch of people there for a card game. Whenever we played cards, Cooter would always buy me in, and then I'd pay him as soon as I was up enough. Tonight we were playing a game called three-card gut, and it was my personal favorite.

Each person is dealt three cards facedown, and the winner is the one with the best hand. The rules make it very interesting. To be able to participate in the next hand, you must roll a card. You can roll a card and still get out of the game safely. However, if you roll a card and it is the highest card rolled, you are in. If you think you have the best three cards and you declare in and you lose, you match the pot. If you win the hand, you are automatically in the next hand without rolling a card. If you don't roll a card, you have to sit out until the pot is right. The pot is right when no one has to double it.

When my trip threes beat Freddy's pair of aces, the verbal assault on me went from bad to worse. He took a long drink from his long-neck Coors Light never taking his eyes off of me and said, "You little sneaky turd. How many more cards you got stashed over there?"

I said, "Keep drinking beer, stupid, and I'll keep taking your money."

Then he told me, "You keep talking, and I will kick you out of that chair."

The night went on like that with Freddy picking everything that I said or did apart. I won enough money to put some gas in my truck and splurge and have an omelet at IHOP for breakfast. As Freddy and Bonnie were leaving, he shot me the finger as they walked out the door. Not long after they walked out of the door leading into the garage, the front door opened.

Freddy walked into the dining room and leaned down over my shoulders and hugged me; he said, "Scoot, you know I love you." As he rose up, he said, "Life is hard."

I said, "Yep."

Freddy popped me on the back of the head and said, "I did not tell you to talk. Life is harder on you. I will not let you get soft."

As Freddy was walking into the garage, I said, "Thanks, brother."

Freddy stopped and looked back at me and gave me a wink.

Dawn and Bonnie sat there sullen faced in Dawn's truck looking at me. I knew they wanted to come and put their arms around me and see what they could do to help me. Like a scared child, I sat there staring into my lap praying that they would leave and not say anything to me. They backed out of their parking space and stopped and sat there looking at me, and I knew they wanted to help. As badly as I needed a kind word, I do not know why it relieved me so much when they drove on.

That night I was sitting on the parking lot of this restaurant on Marshal Avenue watching the people eat and have a good time. My dad and the owner of Pizza King were good friends, and we came here all the time when I was a kid. We came here at least once a week until we moved to Winnsboro, and then it went down to once a month. Hal would always come out of the kitchen to say hello to us.

From time to time, I would run into Hal or his wife somewhere, and they would ask about my mom. I sat there thinking about how Eddie and I used to go pick up sandwiches there when I'd spend the night with him. When Cooter and I would come in from a weekend at Lake Cherokee, we would stop and get pizza for Sunday-night dinner.

Every turn I made in this city there was something that brought back memories that should have made me feel good, but it left me feeling sad. I sat there thinking about all the good times that I had in Pizza King over the years, and it made me so blue. How in the world could anyone with a college degree and a gift of public speaking the way I had end up living this way?

There were so many breaks that most people only hoped for given to me, and this was what they all came to. Two times life slipped away from me, but for some reason, I got another chance. Charles Carson did not get a second chance when he took a job with Domino's to earn cash for Christmas. The three teenagers who kidnapped and killed him admitted they were out to kill a white man that night. The little boy who he left behind is now a proud marine serving in Afghanistan. His daddy will not be there to greet him when he comes home from fighting a war for his country.

One morning, I was drinking coffee getting ready to go to Dr. McBroom's sociology class when the news interrupted the program I was watching with a special report. A Dominos delivery man had been kidnapped and murdered in Dallas last night. The perpetrators of this crime were found the next morning driving the murder victim's pickup. First, they showed a picture of Charles's truck, and a chill went down my spine. Charles was the hardest-working kid I knew besides me, but he never had a car in high school. This truck on the screen in front of me was his first vehicle. Then they showed a picture of the murder victim, and instantly I got sick.

When I walked into the funeral home, the first person I saw was his little brother, Robert Morlan. Robert and Charles had different fathers, but they were all brother. Robert was in bad shape because he and Charles were fighting at the time and had not spoken a word to each other in a while. Charles had quit working for Robert and had taken the job with Dominos because of their fight. Even though Robert had a pretty good reason for being mad, he blamed his brother's death on himself. When Robert looked up and saw me, there were people around him consoling him. He pushed them away, and held out his arms for me to come to him. I had just seen Charles the weekend before. I went home, and as I was driving in, I saw him and Albert crossing the highway. Each of them had a deer on shoulders, and it was in the middle of summer. I went to Robert, and we stood there for what seemed like an eternity crying and holding each other.

Charles's wife remarried a wonderful man that all of Charles's friends have embraced and love. Casey has had a great father figure in his life and has done well because of it. Hardly a day goes by that I do not think about Charles and how very proud he would have been of his son.

Mark Write did not get a second chance when he rolled his jeep. A few months after I had moved to Commerce, I called Cooter.

I said, "What's up, partner!"

Very somberly, he said, "I have been looking for you."

I asked, "What is wrong?"

Then he said, "I don't know how to tell you this."

Not knowing why I asked, "Is Mark all right?"

There was silence for a few seconds before he told me, "Mark is dead."

Mark was killed where he was finishing out his eligibility in Arkansas. The funeral was the next day, and everyone had been looking for me. Vance and I drove to the church in Ore City where the funeral service was going to be. When we got to the church, there was a line fifty yards long leading to the back door to view Mark's body when the service was over. Like the Red Sea parting, the hundreds of people in the line moved out of the way for us.

When the back door of the sanctuary opened for the line to move through, the first person we saw was Mark's dad. Coach Wright had coached his son in high school and had done everything possible to prepare him for the NFL. When he saw me standing there, he broke down and came to me. Coach Wright put his arms around me and walked me to the casket to see his little boy. When I saw Mark, I slipped from coach's grasp and started to fall. Cooter had been standing at the back of the church but somehow managed to catch me.

Steve Tackas did not get a second chance either. Steve and his family were at the rodeo grounds for the Annual Winnsboro Autumn Trails festivities. Steve got in a fight with a drunk who was causing trouble and spanked his butt bad. The drunken man came back with a gun and shot and killed my old friend.

I had let a friend from Winnsboro move in with me, and one afternoon when I came home from work, Ricky was sitting on the couch looking very distraught. Ricky looked at me and said, "You need to sit down."

I said, "Just tell me."

Ricky said, "Scooter, sit down."

When I sat down, Ricky told me, "Steve was murdered yesterday."

Just the weekend before, I had been to Steve and Beth's for lunch and had played with the kids. Steve was a bow hunter, and we had been outside shooting arrows at a Styrofoam target. Steve's son grew up to be a great athlete and is in college now. In a day when nearly everyone has a tattoo, Josh Tackas has a Bible verse on his side. His sister lives and works in Dallas and will probably be getting married soon.

Eddie Berlin did not get a second chance either. I was in the hospital after the second accident when his mom called and told me he had been killed in a motorcycle accident. Later, I went to his grave with Raquel to say good-bye to one of the most amazing friends anyone could ever have had.

Shortly after finding and moving into the house in Oak Cliff, an old friend totally surprised me with a call one night. It was on a Saturday afternoon, and I had spent the day with Ben and his boys just hanging out. After walking home from my old friend's house and turning on the television, my phone started to ring. When I answered the phone, a voice on the other end said, "I have been trying to track down for a long time. Why can you not stay in one place?"

Knowing exactly who this was, I replied, "You are just like Kirkindoll."

Eddie Berlin asked, "Why do you say that?"

Hardly giving him time to finish, I told him, "You nag me just like an angry wife."

Then Eddie said, "I got Raquel to track you down for me."

Thinking back about Eddie's little sister, I asked, "Is she still fine?"

Seriously, he barked back, "Yes, and she is still my sister."

EDDIE

Eddie was in Phoenix going through the program to get certified to be a Harley Davidson mechanic. He told me the next time he came through Dallas on his way to Longview he would stop by. Eddie had been such a good friend to me at Kilgore Junior College. We were not little angels when we got together, but we did have a lot of fun. Eddie had this old four door LTD that everyone affectionately referred to as "The War Wagon." We did most of our running around in it and not on his motorcycle.

Once Eddie had taken me to a football game in Tyler. We were playing Tyler Junior College and I had not got to know any of the football players yet. Eddie had not introduced me to The War Wagon yet, and we actually rode his Harley out of town. He talked the gatekeeper into letting him ride the bike right up to the bleachers so I would not have to walk so far. As he was helping me get off his Harley, a man who worked for the maintenance department walked by on his way to his seat. Everyone on campus knew me already and this man took a good look at Eddie getting me off his Harley and said, "Scooter, you sure are lucky to have such a good friend." Without even looking up or giving it any thought, Eddie told him, "I am the lucky one."

The first time he came home, he took the Hampton Road Exit off of Interstate 30 and showed up at my house pounding on the door screaming, "Open the door. This is the police." Boseman almost chewed a hole through the door trying to get to him. By the time I could get to the window and look out to see what I expected to be one of Ben's friends he was no where in sight. I heard the Harley when it turned the corner near my house and knew it was not a policeman.

I walked out onto the porch to look around. The Harley, and a beautiful one at that, was sitting there but its rider was nowhere in sight. Boseman was on a search and destroy mission. Well if anything was with in the thirty foot radius of that chain, he would destroy it. When Boseman went crazy, Eddie jumped over the rail of the porch and shimmied up the television antenna and was on top of the house. Fearfully he said, "You are going to lock that gorilla in the bathroom or I am not coming down."

I looked up at him laughing and said, "Why didn't you tell me you were coming? I would have put him in his room." All this time Boseman was going crazy. If he thought someone was a threat to me, there was no way I could control him. I kept a chair by the door that I would sit in to connect his chain to let him out. In times like this I could sit in that chair and pull him down from that pole he was trying to climb to get to Eddie.

After I got my dog in the house and locked away in his bedroom, Eddie finally slid down that pole and came inside. The first thing he said was, "How did you make him so mean?"

Smiling I replied, "He has never been that way before." Eddie reached down and picked up the logging chain I put him outside on and said, "I guess your other pet is King Kong." Rolling my eyes I said, "He may be a little mean."

It had been a few years since I had actually seen my old friend. He looked good; just about exactly the same, only his hair was a little longer. We sat down and talked about old times. One night in Kilgore before I moved into the dorms, I was studying hard when there was this pounding on the door. The longer it took me to get there, the harder they knocked. I knew there were at least three people knocking. When I opened the door there was Eddie and James Cashell, John Northcut, Donnie Norvell and they were standing there in the entrance of the duplex passing around the biggest joint I had ever seen in my life.

As soon as I opened the door in rehearsed unison they yelled, "We're going to Shreveport!" They looked like they could not find their way back to Longview, much less to the State Line. Smiling fatherly at them I asked, "Why are you going to Louisiana?"

Eddie poked me in the chest and said, "We means you too."

Pointing to a stack of books on my desk I said, "I have to study."

James asked, "Are you the wise old owl?"

Eddie questioned, "Mr. Owl. How many licks does it take to get to the center of a Tootsie Roll Tootsie Pop."

I said, "Three."

James replied, "You got three minutes to get in the car."

We went to the planetarium to see a light show. As we were approaching our destination we turned this corner and started down the block. About one hundred yards from the corner, a hub cap rolled up beside us and passed us. To say we died laughing would be a gross understatement. Eddie said, "That's my hub cap."

I told him, "Speed up, it's getting away." It had in fact passed us and then howling laughter from the back seat was louder than a rock concert. Donnie exclaimed, "I can't breath make it stop!" If I have ever laughed harder, I do not know when it was. It finally rolled to a stop forty yards from the door of the show. There was a parking place right in front of the door, but Eddie stopped and killed the engine.

After the laughter died down I said, "That was the funniest thing I have ever seen."

Eddie turned to me and said, "Get out and get my hub cap."

That started everyone laughing again. I asked, "Do you want me to put it back on for you?"

Eddie replied, "No put it in the trunk. That was too weird."

Shaking my head I said, "You are a real piece of work."

Stroking his goatee he said, "That's what they tell me."

Eddie decided to spend the night before going on to Longview as long as I kept Boseman locked in his room. We were going to go to my favorite restaurant to eat fajitas and enjoy catching up. Wild Turkey was a cool little spot in North Dallas just off 35. When we get ready to leave Eddie said, "How long has it been since you went for a ride on a Harley?"

Without even thinking about it I said, "Not long enough."

Eddie pleaded, "Come on, bro."

I told him, "We are not kids anymore."

With a look of disgust he said, "You are scared."

We took Westmoreland and while crossing Trinity River Bridge Eddie pulled a wheelie. I squealed like a little girl and begged him to take me home. He was good the rest of the way there, but he scared me bad enough that I took a cab home. On the way home the cab driver crossed over the Trinity and Mockingbird turned into Westmoreland. The driver took a right in to crack hood for some reason that he chose to withhold from me. I asked, "Sir, where are we going?" He said, "It is a pickup." Everyone knew cabs would not even drop off in this neighborhood.

At the first stop sign Eddie rode up beside the driver and hit his door window so hard with the bottom of his fist that I was sure would break. The driver jumped like he had been scalded with hot grease and then looked at me like I was the president. Eddie leaned in and told him, "You are going to 1051 Charmwood." It was fifteen more minutes to my house and Eddie kept that big Harley right beside him all the way. When this remarkable friend left the next morning we both vowed to stay in touch. Eddie was my hero, if he had not taken me in the way he did I may have never been the big man on campus that I was at Kilgore Junior College. He changed my entire life, but he had that effect on everyone. People would tell me I was lucky to have a friend like him and he would always say he was the lucky one.

I was sitting in my living room one night thinking back on all that I had been through. Something I had always thought about and had tried to figure out was what Jeb had said to me the first time I saw him after the accident. I did not remember that I had asked him for a ride home, and he wanted to know if I remembered what the last thing I said to him was. When I asked him what I said he told me, "I'll see you later."

I called Stephanie, and as soon as she answered the phone, I asked her, "Did I ask Jeb to give me a ride home the night broke my neck?"

She took a deep breath that I could hear and said, "I was wondering if you would ever remember. You begged him to take you home."

She told me where he was living and gave me his phone number. After we hung up, I sat there thinking about him and what he had lived with all these years. I had just saw him before the trip and with tears in my eyes had confided in him how hard things were on me at times. I picked up my phone not knowing what I was going to say to him when he answered. When he answered the phone, I said, "This is Scooter."

Jeb said, "What's up, man?"

Wasting no time with pleasantries, I asked, "Did I ask you for a ride home?"

He asked me, "When?"

Without hesitation, I said, "You know when."

Like he really had no clue, Jeb said, "What are you talking about?"

Explaining, I said, "The night of my accident I asked you to give me a ride home."

Feeling trapped, he asked, "Who told you that?"

I answered, "No one told me. I just remembered."

He pleaded, "Scooter, you have it wrong."

Then I said, "If you cannot admit it, there is something I have to say to you."

Surely he thought I was going to be rude by the way he said, "What?"

Releasing every pent-up emotion in my body, I said, "I forgive you."

Before making the call, I had thought about the way he must have punished himself over the years. There was no use in being mad at him because that would only hurt me, and I was sure he had hurt enough. A couple of weeks later, I was in Deep Elum with a friend going to listen to live music. As we were walking up to the club where this local band was playing, Jeb walked around the corner. He walked up to me and put his arms around me and, pressing his mouth on my ear, said, "You are amazing."

There had to have been a reason that I had seen the other side of life and returned twice, other than the relatively few lives that had already been touched. Sitting there smelling pizza and watching all those happy people, I realized that there was a lot left for me to do. Finally, I saw that my life was about more than a place to live or being comfortable. That night, I slept on Sam's Club parking lot on Fourth Street. There was a car wash next to it, and sometimes I parked under the vacuum covers to protect my chair.

Since getting those tickets in Sulphur Springs, I had to be very careful. If for any reason a police officer ran my plates, I am going to jail. As the officer was writing the tickets, I knew that I would end up going to jail over them. One night after a late night in the Aflac Office, I got to my truck and had no idea where to sleep at. I was getting so tired of living this way, and it was taking a toll on me mentally and physically.

I had taken a couple of muscle relaxers about thirty minutes before leaving the office and just wanted to sleep. When I got my chair in my truck, I went ahead and put the cover on it and got back in. After I was back inside, I got a small pillow that I kept behind the console and laid my head over in the passenger seat. I had to wear compression hose because my feet were constantly swelling because of sleeping with my feet on the floor.

Just like clockwork, I awoke at three in the morning and felt of my leg bag. It was full so I sat up and opened my door to empty it.

As I sat there draining my bag, a police car pulled up in front of me, and an officer got out and approached me. He said, "I saw the door of this truck open and am investigating a possible break-in. Can I see some identification?"

I explained, "I work in this building and worked late tonight and fell asleep here."

Shining his flashlight on all of my worldly possessions, he asked, "Where do you live?"

It was getting so hard, and I started to cry. He repeated tenderly, "Son, where do you live?"

I looked at all my things and then back at the policeman. I did not say anything, but my tears were answer enough. He turned and pointed at some cars parked on the back edge of the parking lot and said, "If you sleep here, park over there so you blend in." He gave me his card and, choking back emotion, told me, "This is how you can get in touch with me."

That morning, I went to Whataburger on Gilmer Road to have coffee. The manager of the Fourth Street Whataburger ordered a coffee cup for me with the Whataburger logo on it. It took a few weeks for it to arrive, but with this cup, I got my coffee for twenty-six cents. The overnight shift manager at the Whataburger on the spur would fry me three eggs over easy with toast and bacon. Brent never made me pay either.

I knew the owners of all of the Whataburger's in town from when I went to church at Longview Metro. They had blessed me with five whole dollars for my trip to California. I wanted to get Brent promoted, but I was afraid of getting him fired by telling them how good he was to me.

One Saturday morning, I went to the restaurant next door for breakfast. Juicy's was the home of what is probably the best cheeseburger in East Texas. Brent was off, and I was not going to get a free breakfast or fried eggs at Whataburger. That morning, I was sitting there reading the paper and sipping coffee when Pastor Rob Parsons came in. We talked about me coming back and speaking to the youth at his church. We set up a meeting for the next Monday morning with the new Longview Metro youth pastor.

Jared Adolphus was late, and I had to buy my own breakfast, but the meeting went well. When he sat down, we introduced ourselves, and then I said, "Jared, when I speak to young people, I talk to them about the impact of their choices. Every choice that a kid makes will impact their life."

Jared leaned forward and unconsciously began to draw an ornate cross on a napkin. Being a student of body language, I knew that Jared was hinging on every word I said. Then I leaned forward and said, "I want to tell you a story."

I backed out from the table and pulled along beside him. We were in the Juicy's on Highway 80, and there were two regulars sitting in the same booth they always sat in doing a Bible study. They heard me tell Jared, "Good morning, Pastor."

With Jared and the other two men sitting there waiting for me to speak, I said, "Imagine you are sixteen years old, and you are attending a middle-of-the-week youth meeting with a friend. After the band plays and everyone sings, the youth pastor introduces a special speaker." After I come forward, I tell them, "Everyone, close your eyes and imagine with me. Then I told them, "Then I put microphone close to my mouth and lower my voice.

"Imagine yourself walking down a dark, cold stone corridor. It's dark and dank, and the smell of rotting flesh and raw sewage permeates the air. You have shackles on your feet and your hands are bound tightly. There is a giant of man guiding you—no, steering you by the neck down the long hallway. Then you see the hooded giant swing open a cell door and then shove you inside. The cell door slams, and it is total darkness. Every day, a slot in your door opens, and the guard puts a bowl of gruel and a cup of water inside. As the days turn into weeks your, eyes adjust to the darkness, and you can see the walls surrounding you. The only thing to mark the passing days are your cup of water and stale gruel arriving.

"You begin to make tally marks for the passing days. The time crawls by, and the only light or images exist only in your mind. Finally, one day, the door swings open, and a blinding light hits your eyes. You look away, and the light cast a glow on your walls, revealing thousands of tally marks. You have been in this cell so long that every wall is covered with them. Then you hear a voice say, 'Your bail has been paid and you can leave.'

"You look at your tally marks and think, *I can't leave. This is all I know.* That is what sin will do you it will put you in prison and you cannot get out."

I put my hand on Jared's shoulder and said, "Then I tell them if you don't think sin will put you into prison, open your eyes and look at this wheelchair."

Jared's jaw dropped, and I said, "Now that I have their attention, I tell them my story."

Jared said, "I need to tell my dad about you."

I asked, "Who?"

Jared replied, "I am going to work on a citywide thing for you to speak at. My dad can maybe help you even more though."

One of the men in the booth who had been listening asked, "Can I get your name and number? I am telling my Pastor about you."

Jared and I talked in low voices, and I told him, "For the past year, I have been living in my truck."

Jared put a hand on my shoulder, and his eyes welled up as I continued, "I made a choice that put me in a bad situation." I looked my new friend in the eye and said, "God did not put me in this situation. My bad choices put me here."

Jared said, "Excuse for a moment, I need to call my dad."

When Jared's dad answered, I could hear him just like he was sitting at the table next to us. Jared told him, "Dad, I've got someone here that you are supposed to work with."

His dad asked, "Do I have a choice in this?"

Jerry said, "No, Dad, God is telling me you need to help this man."

I heard Dr. Adolphus say, "All right, when do I meet him?"

Dr. Adolphus has his PhD in divinity from Oral Roberts University and has a company that helps other people in ministry with booking and promotion. That morning, we set up a time in two days for him to come down and meet me. Later that afternoon, I got a call from Pastor Rob.

When I answered the phone, he said, "Son, I need to ask you a question."

I said, "Go ahead."

Then he asked, "Are you sleeping in your truck?"

Knowing Jared had already spilled the beans, I said, "Yes, sir."

Pastor Rob then asked, "Can you meet me at the church at three this afternoon?"

When I got there that afternoon, he took me over to the activity center and showed me around. There were couches and nice furniture with a big kitchen and two big bathrooms. Just when I was wondering what he was doing, he asked me, "Would you start sleeping here? I'll get Pastor Bruce to get you a key."

With a gleam in my eye, I said, "That big leather couch looks comfortable."

That night, I slept on that big couch and slept through the night for the first time in a year. When I got to Whataburger, Brent was actually worried about me. Dr. Adolphus had told me to bring to our meeting Monday if I had anything written about myself so he could read it. I had written a book ten years before but never looked for a publisher. It was written before I had the second accident or started speaking publicly. Leslie had been reading it, and I called her, and she brought it to AK Fitness when she came to work Monday morning.

The bathrooms in the activity center did not have a shower, and after a breakfast of three eggs over easy and grilled Texas Toast with bacon at Whataburger, I headed to AK Fitness to work out and take a shower; as I passed by Leslie's desk, I saw my book. When I lost all my things, it included the computer that my book was on. Alan Bullock's wife had a copy of it on a disk that I had given to her to read. Shelly had two copies made and had them bound in three ring binders and gave me one.

Once before, Debbie Lopez had given me a copy of my book on a disk and an old laptop that she had to bring it up to date on. I spent my days in the library working on rewriting my story. The laptop that she gave me had a bad battery, so I had to be plugged in to be able to use it. It gave me something to feel good about at a time when feeling good was hard to do.

After working on the rewrite for a couple of months, I went to the library one day to finish it. I got my chair unloaded and went into the air-conditioned building to work on finishing my book. I always sat at the same table, if I were not on a computer in the genealogy lab. Today when I plugged the laptop into the wall socket, the power light did not come on. A sick feeling hit the pit of stomach, and I thought, *Why me?*

At least this time if I lost everything that mattered to me, it was backed up on a disk that, for safekeeping, stayed in the D drive of the laptop. The laptop would not come on no matter what I frantically tried. I went to Best Buy and unloaded my chair and went inside to let the geek squad look at it. When I went back to get it, they gave me the bad news that I had feared the most. The man behind the service desk told me, "This laptop is a four-volt but, the adapter that you have been using with it is a nineteen volt."

I asked, "What does that mean?"

He looked at me apologetically and said, "Your laptop is fried."

The worst thing that I imagined could happen have happened. I looked at the store agent and said, "At least I have it backed up on the disk." Then I asked, "Can I have the disk that is in the computer?"

He looked up from the paper he was writing on and said, "There was not a disk in it, sir."

Now the sick feeling in my stomach turned to a burning sensation like I had swallowed a hot coal. When I left the store that day, I went down to IHOP to figure out what I was going to do. My friends who worked there all knew that I was homeless; I had bathed in the bathroom sink too many times for them not to. About many things, I had learned to lose my pride. I could not afford to be proud or to waste anything. If I was eating a piece of chicken and dropped it on a dirty floor, I had to pick it up and eat it. If I had an accident with my leg bag or soiled myself, I had to find a place and go in and clean myself up. This was the hardest blow that I had been hit with since running into that tree.

I was sitting there drinking a glass of tea when Nikki walked by. Sometimes if they were busy and shorthanded, she would come out of her office and be the hostess. She walked by my table with menus in her hand and said, "I'll be right back, Jimmy."

She came back and sat down and asked, "Why do you look so down?"

At that exact moment, Gabe arrived with a plate of strawberry pancakes with a smiley face drawn with whip cream. He sat them down and said, "Compliments of the house."

I thanked Gabe and then looked at the house and said, "You did not have to do that."

Nikki said, "You looked like you needed a smile. What is wrong?"

I took a bite of the strawberry topping that was on my pancakes and said, "My adapter fried my laptop, and I lost the book I was working on."

Nikki took my hand and said, "When it rains, it pours."

I looked up and said, "It will be better when I rewrite it."

She looked into my eyes and said, "I know this has to hurt."

Then I forced a smile and said, "The word says to give thanks in every situation, for this is the will of God in Christ Jesus for you. I feel like crying but will be thankful."

Nikki asked, "What are you going to do?"

I told her, "I am going to wait." She started to ask me what I was going to wait on, and I simply said, "God."

When Dr. Adolphus came into town, we met at Metro Church and talked for about an hour. We were both excited about working together, and after he read my book, he told me that he had connections in Hollywood, and he was already talking to people about a movie. He wanted me to move to Dallas so that I would be near the churches he had me speaking at and the airport.

The first thing he had for me was an Easter service at a church in Arlington. There were thirteen salvation decisions that morning, and that church blessed me with over fourteen hundred dollars. I got a hotel in Terrell because my mother and stepdad live there. It was only minutes away from Dallas, and the hotels in that city that I could afford were not safe.

The next Sunday, he had me at a church in Rockwall, and the altars were full again. After that, I had one speaking engagement at a church on a Wednesday night. Dr. Adolphus did not attend this service, and there was hardly any structure to it at all, and the youth pastor seemed genuinely disinterested with the children there. The youth pastor there was one of the men that Dr. Adolphus worked with, and they were working on getting him the pastor job at the church where I spoke on Easter morning. I even tried to let my mentor know that the kids who had made salvation decisions when I was there were pretty much on their own. When we answer a call and embark upon a life of servitude for God, we are to bloom where are planted until he moves us.

Shelly called me and asked me to come speak at the sports banquet at Winnsboro High School that year. Speaking there was an amazing night, and it was awesome coming back to my high school to talk to my friend's kids. There were actually classmates of mine in the audience. The superintendent was there that night and told me to set something up with schools when the new school year started.

An old friend built a website for me, and I just started doing my own marketing. Francell Burnett had attended the church that I grew up in and was one of my Facebook friends. Dr. Adolphus did not approve on me going on my own to get my website done by an amateur. I do not think he fully understood what the last two years had been like for me. I ate things that men like him would gag on. I did not have thousands or hundreds of dollars to spend on a website. Because I did not blindly follow him or for whatever reason, the man who gave me so much hope abandoned me. I did not have much in Longview, but there was at least a place for me to stay, and I was assured of at least one meal a day. It turned out that the three places he had me speak were all the connections that he had for me.

He got me in front of over thirty people who accepted Jesus as their savior after hearing my testimony. If there had been some warning that the things he was telling me was only empty talk, the money that the Easter service brought in would have been put away. He accomplished what God put him in my life to do, and for that, my heart is grateful.

SAVED BY LOVE

God's strength is made perfect in our weaknesses, and only he knows why things go down the way they do. When Pastor Steve approached after that crawfish boil, he set in motion God's perfect plan for me. The first time I gave my testimony at a youth service at Macedonia Baptist, there were twelve kids who made salvation decisions. Cory and the children's pastor at Macedonia kept me busy after that for a year or so, and every time after that, people gave their lives to God.

The suffering that you are going through and have been such a burden to you can be what sets someone else free. One day, Cory called me and told me he had been asked to speak at an after game pizza party at Tatum High School. When they called him, he thought of me and called to see if I would be interested. We drove down in a church minibus with some of the kids from Macedonia. On the way down, Robbie asked, "What joke are you going to start with?"

I looked back over my shoulder at him and said, "I think I am going to use the chicken joke to open."

From the driver side, Cory looked at me and said, "Why do you think you need to make the kids laugh?"

Then after he turned his attention back to the road, he went on to say, "You have such a powerful testimony, just start with that."

Tatum had played center that night and had beat them fifty six to nothing. The Tatum Eagles went on to win a state championship, and the kids were wound up like the rubber band on a wind-up airplane. After the praise and worship had finished, a local youth pastor introduced me, and I stepped up on a platform in front of fifteen hundred rowdy young people. When I first walked up to the microphone, I thought, *What did I do to deserve this?*

I told a joke, but I do not think one kid in the entire gymnasium heard a single word that I said. Thirty seconds after I started on my testimony and you could have heard a pin drop. As soon as I were through speaking, a youth pastor from one of the churches putting this event on stepped up to the microphone and gave an invitation. A wave of kids rose up from the bleachers and started to come forward, so many kids that it was like Holy Spirit shot me with a cannon. I fell back into the arms of a youth pastor standing behind me. He put me back on my feet and embraced me, and I asked him, "Are they coming for salvation?"

He smiled at me like I had asked him a stupid question and said, "That is what they were called for."

Leaving the gym that night, there was a wet spot on floor where someone had spilled something. I was walking with a cane that night, and my cane slipped out from under me, and I crashed down hard with my left knee taking all of my weight on the hardwood floor. Instantly, I knew that I was hurt bad, and there was no use in trying to get up. Just as quickly as I had fallen, there were kids who had rushed to my side to pick me up. My knee was dislocated, and once they had me up, my left leg was drawn up under me, making me look like a pink yard flamingo.

I stood there for ten minutes unable to lower my knee to the floor thinking we were going to have to call an ambulance. The same youth pastor who had caught me when I fell walked up and said, "Scooter, remember the woman in the Bible with the issue of blood?"

Grimacing with pain and not sure where he was going with this, I replied, "Yes."

Then he told me, "Jesus is passing by. Let's reach out and touch him."

Then he put his hands on my ribs and started praying for me, and all those kids started screaming like crazy. I do not know what the kids were yelling, and I do not know what he prayed, but when he said amen and removed his hands from me, I was standing there on two feet with my kneecap back in place. I believe in healing because over the years, I saw my body go from paralyzed to walking. That was a process in which I worked very hard and without the hard work would have never got on my feet. That night for the first time in my life, I saw an instantaneous, without-a-doubt healing.

Cory and Robbie walked beside me to the door, and then Cory went on to get the bus. We stood there talking, and we watched Cory turn around a start back to us. Cory walked up to me with tears in his eyes and asked, "Did y'all plan that?"

I looked him in the eye and said, "That was all God."

Something happened in my heart that night as well. God showed as much as he used me that he did not need me to entertain; I did not have to tell jokes to hold their attention or anything else. All I had to do was say what God put on my heart and let him do the rest.

Not long after that, Coach Evans asked me to come down and speak to the football team in the locker room before practice one afternoon. I told them the story involving Thomas Everett in the bidistrict football game my senior year in high school. When I finished the story, I said I always wondered when I saw him on television if he remembered that hit. After I was through speaking, one of their coaches approached me, extended his hand, and introduced himself. He was from Dangerfield and had played in that game and told me he knew for a fact Thomas remembered that hit because they had just talked about it.

Even with how God was using me, life was never easy, and the struggle of overcoming homelessness began to take a toll on me. After the money that came in from the few speaking engagements Dr. Adolphus had booked for me was gone, I was back on the streets. A great deal of the money was used on a shopping spree to buy new clothes to speak in, so at least I was the best-dressed homeless man around.

The man whom Mom had married eleven years after my dad had passed away did not always see eye to eye with me, or anyone else for that matter. The thought of going to her house had never crossed my mind as I knew from visits that there was no way to get along with him. It was harder on Mom to know that her son was sleeping in his truck than it was on me. One afternoon, Mom stopped by my hotel room in Terrell, and we discussed the situation that once again I found myself in. She pleaded with me to stay at their house, but deep down with her precious tears rolling down those wonderful cheeks, she knew that was not going to happen.

Mom had just been grocery shopping, and she had some very nice country-cut pork chops that she was going to fry for lunch that day. When she invited me for lunch, she promised mash potatoes, black-eyed peas, biscuits, and gravy to go with them and plenty to go around. There could be no harm in going to Mom's for a country-cooked lunch, and the way things were looking, I would need all the free meals I could get.

My stepfather used a power chair also, and there was a ramp to their front porch which made visits to Mom's house really easy. That afternoon when I got there, while unloading my chair, this voice behind me said, "I was wondering when you were going to come see us."

Turning to look at my stepfather, I replied, "I have been waiting for Mom to fry pork chops."

Rubbing his stomach like he had a tummy ache, he broke the news, "She is going to smother them instead."

The old bait-and-switch tactic had been used on me in the past to get me to their house, so I never said a word about it. Jack could not resist the urge to help me get my chair unloaded, but just as everyone else who tried, he worked against me. Today he was being abnormally nice and was not causing that much extra effort, so I let him help. By the time the harness was removed and my stepfather was out of the way so I could sit down, I heard my mother's voice at the door.

Mom called out to me, "Lunch is almost ready."

My dad had been such a rough and tough man, the kind of man who would come out of a war highly decorated and never tell a soul about it. Military personnel today capitalize on everything possible, and there is nothing wrong with that; it was just such a different mind-set with World War II veterans. My stepfather had managed to stay out of the war, and my dad had lied about his age to get into it. My dad was dying of cancer and had to be alone for weeks at a time because Mom had to be away with her job. My stepfather could not be away from Mom long enough for her to meet me for lunch. The manifold sum of the differences were heavy, and there was no way to ever see him as an equal. However, there were qualities that he possessed that my dad never had until the end. My stepfather was a Christian and worshiped with Mom, and that made her happy.

That day during lunch, my Mom and my stepfather asked me to move into their spare bedroom. The thought of spending any more time sleeping in my truck was heavy on my mind and was a price for my mistakes that I did not want to pay again. I moved into their spare room and stayed in it as much as possible to avoid any conflict that might take place between us. After finally getting Social Security, my benefit amount was only five hundred and fifty-eight dollars a month, and three hundred and fifty dollars came out of that for my truck payment. After things got really bad for me, my stepfather added me to his insurance.

Every time Mom would come into my room to talk, my stepfather would turn the television down so he could try to hear what we were saying. Then out of the blue, one day he assaulted me with a barrage of punches to the face. I was sitting on the couch in the living room talking to Mom, and he came in the room trying to pick a fight. I could have easily overpowered a seventy-nine-year-old man, but I just got up and went outside. The hurt of the whole situation with not having anyone and my own mother not being able to help me was overwhelming. I felt a knot coming up on my right eye and looked at it in the side-view mirror of my truck. Even though his punches were weak and he never hurt me, he had opened up a cut above my left eye.

He once told me that he would not miss an opportunity to have me jailed. He knew that I had shoplifted, and even though it was stealing to eat, this "man of God" was above any thief. Without putting a whole lot of thought into it, I called the police and reported an assault.

As he was being led to the police car in handcuffs, he looked at me and said, "I hope you are satisfied!"

The officer that had stayed outside with me to photograph my injuries told him, "Shut up and get in the car."

At that exact moment, my phone rang, and Vance asked, "What are you doing?"

Looking at the police officer apologetically, I replied, "You are not going to believe this."

He well knew how fragile things were with me and my stepfather, and he asked, "What did he do?"

Defiantly I smirked, "He is being put into a police car with his hands handcuffed behind his back right now."

Through his laughter, Big Vance bellowed, "How many times did he hit you?"

I went back in the house to get a few things and headed to Vance's house at Lake Tawakonee. The next morning, my stepfather called me and told me the judge dismissed the charges and told him to hit me again. A few days after the assault, I came back to get my things; he told me that it was time for me to go down and renew my policy. Cherie Baughman was a friend from high school who was a freight broker and I called logistics companies with freight to move and then found truckers to move the freight for them. I was able to use the wifi at mom's house to do this. There was so much on my plate, but I made a note to call them in the morning.

Vance was on his second marriage and his wife, Amanda, quickly became one of my best friends. They had two sons in high school getting ready for prom night tonight, and I needed to make myself scarce. Their boys were not like we were in high school at all. They were not into partying with friends and drinking until they puked. These were straight-A students, and after the prom, they would be bringing their dates and a few friends to their friend's home.

After leaving my mother's house, I drove the thirty-four miles from Terrell to Greenville to see Amy. I met Amy two days before Christmas at Vance and Amanda's. Amy was Amanda's sister and had the saddest eyes I had seen in a long time. They were the biggest, most beautiful, green eyes I had ever seen, but it looked as though there were an ocean of tears behind them. Both of Amanda's sisters were there that night, and the three of them came walking into the kitchen where I was and asked, "Which one of us are the oldest?"

Feeling the weight of a loaded question, I looked at Amy and said, "She is the oldest, but she is the prettiest."

Amy smiled and said, "I can live with that."

Amy's husband, Roger, was an easy going guy who was always quick to lend a hand if I needed anything. Getting to know them was fortunate because it gave more people in the area to know and hang with. Roger was a good friend to have because he had once worked for a company that sold and repaired power chairs. They invited me over often and I even went to church with them. Amy would always ask me what I wanted to eat and never once did I ask for something that did not seem like her best dish.

That day, I was going to meet her at a restaurant close to where she worked on her lunch break. We had each other in a world of unfairness and deceit. We were still just getting to know each other, but the attraction was all from the heart, and there was little doubt that God had put her into my life. We sat across from each other sipping our waters and eating chips and salsa, talking like two old friends. Amy pulled me from the grips of depression and gave me the will to fight again with a most valued friendship.

Amy asked me, "What are you going to do for the rest of the day?"

Crunching a chip with too much sauce on it, I replied, "Going to McDonald's to write."

Amy reached across the table taking my hand and told me, "I am so proud of you for writing this book. After all that you have been through, you can help so many people."

I turned my hand over and, gripping her hand tightly, said, "The first person I want to help is you."

Amy smiled softly and asked, "How do you want to help me?"

Releasing the death grip I had on her hand and leaning forward a little, I whispered, "To be happy."

Her eyes watered, and tears began to form in the corners of her eyes, and it was the first time I ever saw those sad eyes cry. Then she asked, "Going back to the party tonight?"

She was referring to the after-prom party at Vance and Amanda's house. The last thing those kids needed at their prom party was me, and I said, "I am going to rent a room tonight."

Amy made a sad face and asked, "I know they would love to have you there."

Knowing this was a time for family, I replied, "I just want to lie in the middle of a big bed in my boxers and watch television."

Amy got serious and inquired, "Are you really getting a hotel?"

Then she added, "I know Bryce and Casey will want you there." Casey was Bryce's best friend and was State Power Lifting Champion. This kid was so humble about it and so filled with the love of Christ. I would watch him and Bryce come in after school and make a sandwich and sit at the table to eat. Before they would take a bite they would each bow their heads and not just bless their food, but pray earnestly. I envied them. Not because they had each achieved so much, but because they had a genuine relationship with God as teenagers. That did not guarantee an easy life, but it would sure keep them from the pain of mine.

Actually I had no intention of getting a hotel when I was going to have to renew my insurance, but I did not want her to worry about me. I had slept in my truck so many times that one more night would be nothing.

We sat there eating lunch and talking about many of the things in my book and her life. Every conversation we had started with me saying, "Tell me a story."

Sometimes in a cute, dainty voice, she would say, "I don't know a story."

Most of the time she would squint her eyes and crinkle her lips and think hard to come up with some story about herself to tell me. I loved hearing about her, and she was the same with me. Her eight-year-old daughter was a mini-version of herself and was just as beautiful. Amy was a tall, five feet ten inches, with blond hair and those beautiful, green eyes. When I met her, she had just lost fifty pounds and was extremely self-conscious about her weight. She was so modest and had no idea how beautiful she was, and that was a great deal of her allure.

That night, I stayed at McDonald's until the dining room closed and then headed to Wal-Mart to spend the night. Wal-Mart parking lot was always a good place to sleep if you got in a far out of the way corner. However, not too far and out of the way or you would not be safe. Normally, there would be an eighteen-wheeler or two camped out on a Wal-Mart parking lot, and it was safe to park close to them. With my wheelchair in the back, truckers were good about watching out for me.

On this particular night, it was so hot, and my gas was running too low to run the engine and the air conditioner. Even on a parking lot that is well lit, it is not a good idea to leave your windows down far enough for someone to get their hand inside. If I could just get through the night and the heat, the safety of the morning sun would allow me to lower a window and get some sleep. Tossing and turning is not easy to do in the seat of a truck, and I have a scar the size of a palm print on my right side from where the seatbelt connector stabbed me in the side every night. Most nights I covered it up with a jacket or something, but my sensitivity in my right side is decreased, and even then it was doing damage. At five o'clock in the morning, I had not been to sleep even for a few minutes and decided to drive down to McDonald's and drink a cup of coffee.

Delirium was the best word to describe my state of mind at that time, with the lack of sleep and all of the other stressful things in my life eating away at my peace of mind like flesh eating bacteria. With my truck moving and both of the windows rolled halfway down, the cooler morning air was not stagnant, and it relaxed me instantly. With my left hand resting on top of the steering wheel and my torso slumped toward the console, my right elbow held me up like a giant steel girder. This was the most comfortable I had been all night, and soon I was drifting off to sleep.

I knew that I was asleep, but at the same time, I could feel the rolling wheels under me. Just then I heard this air horn blow a long, sustained blast, and I knew I was headed for danger. Opening my eyes and rising up, I saw that I was in the ditch of the Interstate 30 service road headed straight for a big metal utility pole. Sharply cutting the steering wheel to the left to avoid the pole, I watched it sheer off the right front end of my Silverado. When my truck slammed into the embankment on the other side of the ditch, my power chair crashed into the back of the cab and flipped out of the truck. Surely it was demolished, but I never saw it again. If the truck driver who pulled that long blast one his air horn had not alerted me to the approaching pole, there would have been no surviving this crash. That big metal pole would have sliced through my truck and me like a missile through a swimming pool.

I am not sure if the airbag was faulty or if the force of the crash threw me forward so hard it made it pop. This hole the size of a fifty-cent piece blew out of the bag right in front of me. The tear was spewing steam like a teapot boiling over, and the edge around it caught on fire. There were sparks flying and a fire starting in the dash that I could not get to, but I beat the airbag fire out with the palm of my hand. In a matter of seconds, it seemed a man opened my door and reached over me with a fire extinguisher and put the dash fire out.

From the examining table in the emergency room using my cell phone, I called Vance to come get me. After he got to the hospital, he used a hospital wheelchair to get me from the lobby to his car. This was going to be a devastating blow to me to be stuck on Vance's couch with no way to get out of the house even for a few minutes would be miserable for me and them. After we were on our way back to his house, I called Allstate to report my accident and cut that time down as much as possible. It was not time to renew my policy at all as my stepfather told me; he had canceled my insurance three weeks earlier. Before he had even gone to jail for assaulting me, he had removed my truck from his policy. I lost everything I had of any value because he did not just tell me the truth. My truck, my lift, and my wheelchair were all gone when a phone call would have established coverage if he had only told me.

Two days later, I was sitting on the patio at Vance's house drinking coffee looking out over the lake, wondering what I was going to do. Vance had been looking for another coaching position and had recently taken a job in Corpus Christie—a good three hundred and seventy miles away. It was going to take awhile to get a leg brace, and I did not have any business walking without one. Luckily for me, there was a walker in their garage that I had left a few weeks before. The kids were getting ready for school, and mostly I was on the patio to stay out of their way. The back door opened, and Vance told me if I wanted to get ready, he would take me up to the Quinlan McDonald's so I could use their Wi-Fi and work booking freight. He had to run an errand before he went to the high school where he was a coach. I had thirty minutes to get ready, so after taking the last few sips of my coffee, I got up and headed inside.

I got inside the back door and sat my walker down in front of me and turned around to shut the door behind me. I got off balance in the turn and fell to my weak side. In a last-ditch effort to keep from hitting the floor, I lunged toward the wall to stop my fall. I heard the two bones in my right lower leg right above the ankle snap before I hit the floor. There was no doubt in my mind that I had just broken my leg in what seemed to be the simplest of falls. I used my good hand to pick my right leg up, and the ankle dropped like a dangling participle.

The pain was excruciating, but there were Vance's children to think of, so I had to hide my irritation. The first one to see me on the floor was Hunter. He was eleven years old and was Vance's youngest stepson. One day out of the clear blue, he started calling me Lieutenant Dan; in return, I called him Forrest. Hunter ran to me and asked, "Are you all right?"

Grimacing in pain, I said, "Go get Bryce."

Hunter ran to the stairs and bounding upward called out to his stepbrother, "Bryce, Lieutenant Dan is hurt."

Bryce and Dakota came flying down the stairs and ran to the back door where I lay. Bryce took one look at my leg and turned to Dakota and said, "Go outside and wait for the ambulance."

He took out his cell phone called an ambulance and then got down on a knee and put his hand on my leg and began to pray for me. I was so proud of Bryce and Dakota and the men that they were becoming. I had actually been at the hospital when Bryce was born and stood next to Mr. Hale the first time he saw his grandson. Watching that kid grow up has been an honor because he was so different from me and Vance. He and Dakota both are born-again Christians and faithfully attend church. They are both straight-A students, and Bryce was selected to the Academic All-State High School Football Team. This fall, he begins playing his sophomore year at East Texas Baptist University in Marshall, Texas, on a full scholarship.

Until the ambulance arrived, he never left my side. Lying there on the floor, I sent a text message to Amy to let her know what had happened. She was working but took an unscheduled break and called me. The first thing she asked was, "Are you all right?"

I told her, "I am so sorry."

Perplexed she asked me, "Why are you sorry?"

Taking a deep breath and trying not to start sobbing, I assured her, "For putting you through so much."

She was tearful when she asked, "What do you mean?"

Laying it all out like she was holding my paralyzed hand and hanging on every word, I went on, "All those years I begged God to send me an angel to get me through. Now in the darkest hour here you come."

Amy, with a clearly shaken voice, asked, "Why are you doing this to yourself?"

In a panicked voice, I cried, "I don't want to lose you."

I could hear the smile in her voice when she said, "You will never lose me."

Just then Dakota came walking in with the ambulance crew, and I had to hang up. On the way to the hospital, she called me back and asked, "Where are they taking you?"

They had just asked me if I wanted to go to the hospital in Rockwall or Greenville. Naturally, I had chosen Greenville so that I could be close to her, so I replied, "Hunt Regional."

Amy said, "As soon as I get off of work, I will be there. I will be praying for you."

Dr. Chun was my orthopedic surgeon, and it was a good thing because he was top-notch. Before he operated, he came by to talk to me about my options. Because of my spinal cord injury and decreased circulation in my right leg, he was very hesitant about operating. If for some reason an infection set in, there was a high probability that he would have to amputate my leg. The way the tibia was shattered, if he put it in a cast, it would never heal. There was not really any thought that went into my decision to tell him to operate.

He put two plates and twelve screws in my leg to repair the fractured tibia and fibula. The shattered tibia was a little more complicated than a plate and some screws. He took all the pieces out and ground them into powder and mixed them into a paste to form a new bone. This operation took five and a half hours. To stave off an infection, they kept my so full of antibiotics if you would have shot at me with a high-powered rifle, the bullet would have veered around me.

When they brought me into recovery, true to her word, Amy was there waiting for me. We were talking when my cell phone rang, and it was my mom. I answered, "Hey, Mom."

She said, "You'll never guess where we are."

To which I replied, "Guess where I am."

Without a guess, Mom told me, "We had to go to court today over the assault charge."

Remembering my stepfather's braggadocios call about the judge telling him to hit me again, I said, "I thought those charges were dropped."

Mom cried, "He was confused, son. He is getting two to ten years. They charged him with felony assault."

Then I asked, "Why are you telling me this, Mom?"

Still sobbing, she said, "His lawyer has an affidavit for you to sign, and they will drop the charges."

Just then I thought about losing my truck and my power chair along with a lift just because of his meanness. My truck added $56 in premium because my wife and I were on her policy which was old and cheap. As soon as got my disability I started paying him my monthly part of the bill. Then I thought about all the second chances I had received and the fresh starts. I thought about Amy and the grace that she was so accomplished at giving out. I thought about what I had done to deserve the friendship of this beautiful woman who was standing beside me and could come up with nothing. The only thing that I could possibly do to merit such unwarranted favor was to be Christ-like and give my stepfather a break. Even if he never would acknowledge it as a favor or a turned good deed, I had to do it.

I said, "Send the lawyer to Hunt Regional Hospital in Greenville, and I will sign the paper."

Mom asked, "You are not at Vance's house?"

Explaining I said, "I broke my leg and just got out of surgery."

Mom said, "Maybe I can make it over there one day next week."

Amy was there for me every day through thick and thin. She washed my clothes for me, and she and her eight-year-old daughter would come at night and watch television with me or play games. As irony would have it, her daughter's name was Grace, but everyone called her Gracie. I taught this beautiful little girl my favorite scripture: "God resists the proud but gives grace to the humble" (James 4:6). Breaking my leg brought us all together in a way I never thought possible. Exactly thirty days after fracturing the tibia and the fibula, I fell getting into my wheelchair and split the tibia from just below the knee down to the first plate on the original fracture. Lying there on the floor with my leg broke in three places, the only thing I had to be thankful for was Amy. That made a lot more sense than crying. This was the most frightening time in my life, and had it not been for a woman whom I had just met, I would be facing that fear alone.

Out of the hospital I went to a place called *Legends* for my rehabilitation. I had this physical therapist I referred to as the water girl. Whenever it came time for us to do therapy, she spent half of that time getting other patients drinks of water. I went to the Social Worker and explained that I was homeless and needed help finding housing. Connie got her Rolodex and asked me if I had a cell phone. I told her yes and she looked up a few numbers. After she had written them down, she gave me the list and said, "Call these places."

After breaking my leg the second time, when I came back from the hospital I had another physical therapist. Helmut really knew what he was doing and we got along great. I thought the head of therapy there was a pain and butted heads with her almost every day over the stupidest stuff. The same with the Assistant Director of Nurses. Between the two of them and all the social services that were provided to me, I began to look for another place to live. Holly and her best friend Megan were aides that were my best friends there. They gave me a hard time about leaving.

Helmut was the only really good thing about Legends. I had friends there but everything was rules and they were all so uptight. The building was awesome and I bet they had twenty thousand dollars worth of furniture in the vestibule. An amazing new building with a private room was not enough to diffuse the strife created by those three people. Helmut gave me the idea to check out Greenville Health and Rehabilitation.

I got the number from information and called to see about a tour. Sarah, the recruiter, was not in, so I left my number for her to call me back. Someone at Legends told me they referred to it as Greenville Death and Rehabilitation. When Sarah and Dianne came to pick me up in the bus, I was sure that I was not going to like what I saw. As the bus pulled up to pick me up there was an uneasy feeling in my stomach. I did not want to do something rash and regret it later.

The door of the bus opened and the vivacious brunette with an attitude stepped off and said, "Are you Jimmy?"

I took one good look at her and replied, "Do you want to just go ahead and load my stuff?"

With a backhand gesture she said, "Are you going to be a problem? Get on the bus."

She sounded like Bugs Bunny doing Rambo, so in my best Elmer Fudd I said, "Are you this way with everyone or am I special?

Right away we were friends and the place was looking better than it sounded. The ride over on the wheelchair equipped bus was like an eight second ride on a bull named Fu Man Chu. The facility was right across the street from the hospital and the charge nurse on the seventh floor was a buddy and I knew at least he would visit. All me and Amy were was really good friends but it got to where I saw her and Gracie less and less.

As the bus pulled up to the building a fading feeling hit my stomach and the phrase *Greenville Death and Rehab* jumped out at me like cold sore on a fat lip. The building looked like it was fifty years old and there was this five hundred pound man sitting under the awning He was in a very big wheelchair and we waited for the man to move and Sarah told me, "That's Joe, he has been here for a few months."

Then she said, "He is so sweet."

As soon as I got off the bus at the speed of smell I made my way over in my manual chair to say hello to Joe. He had his head down trying to avoid any eye contact. I reached over and put my hand on his arm and said, "Hey buddy."

He never said a word so I asked, "Are you enjoying this day?" Then he replied, "The sun feels good."

Then I told him, "My name is Jimmy."

Thinking he would tell me his name I was surprised to hear him ask, "Have you ever been to New Jersey?" Taken aback I told him, "Not yet, but I hear it is nice." Finally looking at me Joe said, "It's the most beautiful place on earth." Then I said, "You must be from there." In turn he asked again, "Have you been there?" Knowing what I was up against now I said, "No but I hear it is the most beautiful place on earth."

Sarah was at the door smiling at me, but I knew she was ready to start her tour. I explained to Joe that I had to go check out the facility and he asked excitedly, "Are you going to live here?" I asked him, "Would you like that?" With a smile bigger than New Jersey he said, "That would be so cool."

The only thing I really cared about seeing was the physical therapy room. Before starting on the tour we stopped at the office and I met the administrator and the lady who did the payroll. They were super nice and the label *Greenville Death and Rehab* was slipping away. The nursing facility was laid out in four wings or halls just like Legends. Amy worked as a medical coder and she said even they referred to it as *Greenville Death and Rehab.* The only thing I can figure that would warrant that name being issued to this facility is the age of the building. The people there were the best I had ever been around in a hospital setting. It is important to remember that I had spent five years of my life in hospitals. The main reason I came here in the first place was Joe; I figured he needed a friend.

The cafeteria there was much better than the food at most hospitals half the time. These ladies had spent their lives cooking soul food and they gave my mother, who is an amazing cook, a run for her money. Chastity, the dietary manager, would always hook me up with just about anything I wanted within reason. In my first thirty days here I gained twelve pounds. Which is not a good thing when you are trying to walk again. Amy was a distributer for Visalus and I got a thirty day supply from her and started doing a shake for lunch and dinner. Visalus is relatively new on the scene but it is how Amy lost her weight, so I figured to give it a try.

My first roommate was Michael Smith. He was six years younger than me, but one of my nurse friends told me he was terminally ill. Michael's wife left him and took his son and in turn he took to drinking whiskey and a lot of it. He told me he liked the cheap stuff. He would rather drink rot gut whiskey over anything. He told me he came to a point where he was drinking a half gallon a day, but his cousin told me it was closer to a gallon.

The aides would walk in the room with his food and ask him if he was hungry. His body was full of bile and toxins and naturally he was not hungry but he needed to eat so I started feeding him. One night I was sitting beside him feeding him a subway pizza and asked, "Do you believe in heaven?"

Michael replied, "Yes."

Then I put the pizza down and took his hand. He turned his head to me and looked at me as if he were longing for something. I asked him, "Michael, are you going to heaven?"

He had closed his eyes, but he opened them and said, "I don't know."

Holding his hand tightly I said, "Buddy, there are angels all around you right now."

His eyes were averted but he looked at me and I went on, "Do you want to go to heaven?"

He looked at me pleadingly and said, "Tell me how."

I said, "Michael, it is so easy. Do you believe that Jesus was the son of God and that he died on a cross for the remission your sins?"

He nodded his head and I said, "Say it. Confess it with your mouth."

Through his labored breathing he told me, "I believe Jesus was the son of God and he died for my sins."

Then I asked him, "Do you believe that after three days he rose again and is seated at the right hand of God?"

This time he said with newfound strength, "After three days he rose from the dead."

Then I asked, "Do you receive him into your heart as your personal savior?"

Michael's eyes opened wide and he said, "Come into my heart and save me, Jesus."

Two days later I went across the street to eat breakfast and to get Michael a donut. He told me that he would eat a glazed donut if I got him one. I had kept an around the clock vigil with him because knew the end was near, As I entered the door of Greenville Health and Rehabilitation a lady from the business office named Tameko was waiting on me. As soon as I came through the door she said, "Jimmy, will you come with me?" She was my friend so I said, "Sure." Then she started walking towards the room where my friend and Christian brother lay dying. I pulled up along beside her, looked up, and with cracking voice said, "I was only gone for a few minutes."

She said, "Jimmy, do not feel bad. You have no idea what you meant to that man."

I came to love Michael and was very protective of him. He did not have an appetite at all, and I am sure I prolonged his life by a few weeks by bringing him Subway sandwiches. I called a pawnshop here in Greenville and asked if they had a power chair for sale. They had one that had been in their storeroom for five years. He told me he would let me have it for $200, but then he made me pay for the new batteries it needed. I should have called Rick at American Pawn. With the power chair, I was able to get out and go my visit my friend Sonny at the hospital. Sonny is the Charge Nurse on the seventh floor of the hospital Hunt Regional Hospital. Sonny worked with me each time I had broken my leg.

After Dr. Chun operated on me the first time, he put a plate and twelve screws in my ankle. The first break, the tibia and the fibula were broken right above the ankle. The tibia was shattered, and he took the pieces out and ground them into a paste to form a new bone. I was very fortunate to have such a good doctor working on me. In the second break they called him, but he was out of town until Monday. He told them to take me to a hospital in Dallas to another orthopedic surgeon.

I told them I would wait until Monday. I woke up a few hours later and the good doctor was standing there preparing to cast my leg. After my entire leg from foot to groin was casted, I was moved to a recovery room for a few days. Then they moved me up to the seventh floor for rehabilitation and I met Sonny Rogers. We were definitely two peas in a pod and instantly became friends. He had even went to high school in Winnsboro for one year. You might say we had some stuff in common.

The cafeteria at the hospital was known for a great breakfast, and I was there eating a one pound omelet every morning. The bag of Visalus shake mix sat on my dresser untouched for a month. The day I weighed in at 232 pounds I wiped the dust off the bag and gave it some serious thought. By this time it had been three months since I had seen Amy and soon I was gaining so much weight. We still talked by text nearly every day.

Vance had taken a coaching job at Calallen high school in Corpus Christi and I had no place to go. Joann, the social worker at this facility knew what she was doing. The first thing she did was get me qualified for Community Based Assistance. That was a program that helped people move back into the community from a long term care facility. They provided a client with $3500 for furniture, dishes, appliances, housewares and deposits. This is a lot of money to invest in someone, and they want to be sure you will make it.

With me being in a long term care facility, I got on the short waiting list with The Department of Housing and Urban Development or HUD. The normal waiting list is two years, but with me having CBA and being in a rehabilitation facility it was cut down to three months. As the time drew near for me to be able to get out, I went to the social worker's office to check on how close I was to being able to leave. To my dismay the funds for HUD had been frozen and there would be no housing voucher for me. If there was going to be a roof over my head, it was going to be as a long term resident at Greenville Health and Rehabilitation.

The only time I did not feel like crying was when I was on the Nustep working out. I pushed as hard as humanly possible to push the pain out of my heart. Sometimes I went all out for an hour, but most of the time it was thirty minutes. However long I went, it was as hard as I could go. I worked with all of the therapists and earned the respect of each one of them.

John Varnell was one of my Facebook friends and we talked nearly every day. Once I posted a picture of a bag of Visalus shake mix that Amy had given me and a carton of milk with the caption "dinner." Before long I got a message from John telling me about his friend Sheryl Lau. She was a Regional Director with Visalus, and after we met she sponsored me so I could get my product for free.

With the Visalus shake mix in the first month I lost ten pounds with Sheryl helping me with my diet. I would have two shakes a day and two modest meals. Over the next six weeks I gained eight pounds of muscle and every bit of respect Sheryl had to give. So much so that she made me a promoter for her business. Sheryl helped me to focus again and that was something terribly needed.

Even when I was a kid and an athlete in high school I had a belly and never a stomach. It felt so good to have a tight stomach and to be working on six pack abdominal muscles. I have never known of or even heard of a quadriplegic with a six pack. It may take years, but with working out and eating right I would not bet against me.

Amy had not abandoned me at all. She had her own problems to deal with and even though she was not here, she would text. During our time apart we spent more time praying for each other than we probably would have spent together. The old adage "absence makes the heart grow fonder" was definitely true in my case. Sometimes when you are without something for so long and then all of a sudden you have it, you do not have the appreciation for it you should. I thought I did, but in reality the only appreciation that I really had was for the way she made me feel about myself. Consideration for her needs fell aside and I began to feel like it was her duty to run my errands and wash my clothes and be all of the emotional support I had. I learned there are things in life to perfect to take for granted.

I had stumbled upon an orchid beaten down by the weather of life and too delicate to touch. I loaded her down with duties and obligations and it got to be more responsibility than she could bear. By the time we started talking again, I was spending two hours a day on a step machine with it on the hardest level in hopes that my tortured heart would stop. This one lesson drove me closer to God than I have ever been in my life. When you have someone in your life who makes a difference, be the difference in their life too. Jesus said his followers would be the light of the world. We are called to be Jesus to everyone we meet with our love light. Amy placed spotlight of love on my path that pulled me out of the dark.

People need love, the kind of love Jesus gave when he said, "Father, forgive them for they know not what they do." The same kind of love Amy showed me when she would get off of a long day of work and drive twenty-two miles roundtrip to get Gracie and come back and have dinner and play games with me. Thank God for people like that and give that kind of love in return; chances are they need it more than you.

Compared to Legends, Greenville Health and Rehabilitation was like going from Park Avenue to the slums of Calcutta if you just looked at the building. There was such a relaxed atmosphere there and the business manager there assured me that when my Medicare days ran out, they would switch me over to Nursing Home Medicaid and keep me. Legends had actually put me out with a full cast on my right leg because I had reached the end of Medicare Eligibility. Jack had let mom come up and get me into a cheap hotel, but he would not let her bring me home to stay with them. It took my mom, her friend, and two nurses just to get me into the car. When we got to this hotel and I got into my chair, we had to wait on the maintenance man to build a ramp for me to get over the threshold. There would be no way that I would be able to navigate this ramp by myself.

Mom brought me some canned goods that she got from her church, and my room at the Travel Lodge had a small refrigerator and a microwave. She brought a little crock pot and a big bag of dry pinto beans. I had stopped a lady with a home health agency in the hall at Legends one day and told her that I was going to need assistance. Totally on my own and apart from any help from the social worker at Legends, I struggled and suffered to make it. It was three days after leaving Legends before the home health people were able to get me a hospital bed and a potty chair. Life had not been this hard even when I was homeless. I could not get into the bathroom at all and had to bathe out of a sink that I could barely reach. The only thing I could do with my urine was run the water and pour it down the sink. The same sink I washed my dishes and got drinking water from I was forced to use as a urinal.

One day after she got off work Amy stopped by to check on me. I had already asked her not to bring Gracie because I did not want her to see the way I was living and it was unsafe to let her stay outside. Amy came in and I just started crying. As soon as she saw the first tear, she started crying as well. I was sitting in my wheelchair and she walked over to the table and got a chair and pulled up beside me. Sobbing almost uncontrollably I said, "I do not know how I am ever going to get on my feet."

As Amy sat there talking to me she looked down at my cast and screamed, "Oh no, Jimmy!" Then she said, "We have got to get you to the emergency room!"

Thinking she was over reacting over a sunburn I asked, "Why do I need to go to the hospital?"

Taking a deep breath she calmed down a little before saying, "You have a severe case of cellulitis."

Never having even heard if it I asked her, "Is that bad?"

With the compassion and love that could only come from a mother's heart she said, "I am calling 911, this looks very bad." Then she told me, "We have got to get you an ambulance."

I had the maintenance man get me out of the room in the afternoons and I would sit on the sidewalk in the afternoon sun. I thought my glowing red toes cascading from the cast like molten lava from Mount Saint Helens were sunburnt. The attending physician in the emergency room told me that the infection was in my blood and if I had not came in, my blood would have turned septic and within twenty four hours I would have been dead. Amy would never take credit for saving my life, but any way you look at it she is the only reason people will read this book.

Hunt Regional Hospital kept me for ten days treating a severe case of cellulitis, that in the words of my good friend Sonny Rogers, was about to get nasty. The cast came off that first day in the emergency room so I was able to get up on the seventh floor and do a little rehabilitation work. Sonny made it like a vacation almost and I pleaded with them to let me stay. The second time I broke my leg I was at Legends. I was getting out of bed into my wheelchair early one morning and the pocket of my sleep pants hung on the break. The facility was amazing but the therapy was not even average. I went back there because of familiarity and Holy Ann. Even Gracie had fallen in love with her.

The morning of the second break, I was transferring from my bed to my wheelchair and the pocket of my sleep pants got hung on the brake. I hung there, suspended in time like the tail on a kite, knowing that without help I was going to fall. My door was open and I began to call out and with my room being right across the hall from the nurse's station, I thought I had a pretty good chance at getting help. When I was still laying down, I could see that there was a nurse sitting across the hall at the desk of the substation. My left side is my strong side and my head was leaning to the left. I was trying to use those muscles to keep from going down. My chair was beside the bed facing the foot of the bed and I was transferring to my left. I called out and hung on as long as possible. When my butt slipped off the bed, my head and my legs went left, but my butt went right. On the way down I heard what reminded me of timber cracking, a sound that reluctantly I heard to many times as a kid cutting winter firewood.

Laying there on the floor I knew that this break was bad. I heard that nurse sitting outside at the desk tell an aide, "Please check on Mr. Drew. I think he needs help." When she walked in the room I told her, "Call an ambulance. I just broke my leg." The tibia was split from just below the knee down to the plate Dr. Chun had fixed the first break with.

When I transferred to Greenville Health and Rehabilitation and got my power chair, there were things close by for me to investigate. All I had to do was go to the nurse's station and sign out. There was a Valero on the corner that had a Subway restaurant inside where I frequently loitered. I was in there so much that I got to know the owner and his family.

One day Steve Ash was sitting with me having a cup of coffee and he said, "Jimmy, you should buy this store from me." I figured he was pulling my leg and said, "Who do I make the check out to?" Steve replied, "If you want it, we'll figure something out."

I was there every morning because of the coffee. They only served decaffeinated coffee in the cafeteria and that was not ready until 7:30, and I needed coffee when I woke up. To keep me from venturing out on the streets of Greenville before the sun came up, the two administrative nurses put a coffee maker in their office just for me. The bad thing about it was that Gina came in at eight and Tammy was an hour later. I hung out in there so much we called it my office.

There was a room off the main entrance of the building with a big flat screen on the wall. There were also a couple of couches and two big chairs, and in the back corner of the room there was a piano. This was Joe's favorite room and just about any time of day you could find him sitting on one of those couches with the remote in his hand asleep. After I had been there for a few days, Joe told me that I was the best friend he ever had.

One night Joe was telling me about all the wonders of both New Jersey and AC/DC. Those were his two loves and he would not let anyone forget it. Very animatedly Joe told me, "New Jersey is the most beautiful place on earth!"

I replied, "Texas is beautiful."

To which he said, "This place is a desert."

I thought about it and told him, "I am going to start calling you Jersey Joe."

His smile was almost as big as he was and he said, "I like that."

Joe's mother had passed about twenty years ago and he had been living in another facility not far away. Joe was so innocent but easily annoyed people who did not have the patience for his repetitive childish questions. They used me as an ambassador with Joe with delicate matters. The most delicate of which was getting him to shower. One night I asked Joe if he believed in heaven and he told me he did. When I asked him if he was going he told me he had not decided. In the simplest way I could, I told him about Jesus and the cross. Joe prayed and received salvation.

I had been to Joe's room a few times before, but the next day went down to give him a Bible. Joe had the wall beside his bed covered with two AC/DC posters and pages of pictures of New Jersey that were torn out of magazines. When I got there I saw a new addition to the wall. He had taken a sheet of paper and with a blue ink pen had scribbled in bold letters, "Jersey Joe's AC/DC wall Poetry in motion." When I saw that, instantly I thought about how much God had used me since I had been here. No matter what your situation is, you can make a difference in someone's life if you will bloom where you are planted.

Because Jack took my truck off of his policy without telling me, there was still a three-hundred-and-fifty-a-month car payment to be made to the bank. My sweet friend had gone way beyond the expectations of any banker to keep me driving that truck. Once Julie told me that if the truck belonged to anyone else, it would have gone back to the bank a long time ago. There was no way that I could stop making payments, even though the truck was a total loss. The front axle and through to the passenger door was sheered in half where the utility pole passed through it with surgical precision that even Dr. Chun would have been proud of. There were not any major dents; only the right front portion of the truck was sliced off. Had it not been for that last second jerk of the wheel, that pole would have passed right through me. Jan and Julie went to work getting the bank's insurance to pay my truck off. After it was all said and done, there was still a little more than a couple of thousand dollars because of premiums for a backdated policy and storage fees where my truck was impounded. They had refinanced it for me so many times that there was still over ten-thousand-dollar balance the bank's insurance paid off.

Eighty-five days after breaking my leg the first time, I walked with a platform walker. A platform walker has an extension on one side, or a platform to rest your arm on. Since my right arm was weak, the platform was on the right side. It consisted of a place to rest my arm with a hand grip sticking up at the end of it. By putting my weight on my elbow of my right arm and locking the elbow straight on my other arm, I was able to hop on my left leg.

After getting the cast off and moving to Greenville Health and Rehabilitation, I was walking every day but my right leg would start to spasm so bad that I could not go very far. When I would stand to do weight shifts my hips would hurt so bad that I could only take a few minutes of the pain. One day I went into the therapy room to talk to the head of the department. I pulled up beside Steve and said, "I am beginning to think I will not functionally walk again without that double hip replacement." Steve told me, "I know that doctor told you that you needed that, but it is the last thing you want." I shook it off and said, "It looks like I am going to need a new power chair."

A few days later Steve came to my room after my morning workout with a man who I did not know. When I would get on the Nustep I gave it everything that I had to give. After I got off, I went strait to bed and collapsed until the afternoon workout. When Steve knocked on my door, I said, "Go away." He opened it and walked in and said, "Make me." Then he said, "This is Billy and we are trying to get you approved for a new chair."

The chair they got me is the Bentley of power wheelchairs. The legs on it raise and the back fully reclines. This is all done with the hand controls, so other than pushing a button there is no effort on my part. I could have been bitter about not being able to walk any longer; but instead I chose to be thankful for my life which had been spared so many times. Because of my thankful heart, I was blessed with a $22,000 wheelchair. When they delivered it they told me that it was a $40,000 chair. They got the chair down that low to get me approved and let me tell you this; it really is a $40,000 power chair. Steve set my inside speed to 1 mile per hour maximum. That is really creeping at turtle speed but with elderly people walking on walkers, I have to be respectful.

They delivered the chair on a Friday and it gave me the weekend to get used to it. Steve set my inside speed and the speed I could use on the hospital grounds. When I was going anywhere off the grounds I could open it up full speed a blazing 6 miles per hour. Monday there was an appointment with my neurologist, who was trying to figure out where all of the spasticity in my right leg was coming from. Dr. De Jesus's office was right around the corner. It was directly across from the hospital emergency room in the same complex as Dr. Chun's office.

On my way back I saw the Director of Nursing standing out by the back patio watching me. Upon entering the parking lot immediately I stopped to gear down to grounds speed. I heard Terri say to an aide beside her, "Look, it took him twenty feet to get shut down." When you let off of the stick the chair will roll anywhere from one to three feet, depending on how fast you are going. I knew this was going to be trouble the way she was angrily approaching me. The first thing she said was, "You do not even have you seat belt on."

Clasping it with my thumb and snapping it back to my waist band I said, "This is the seat belt you are referring to."

I went inside to lay down and woke to a knock on the door. Steve came in and said, "You have got to be super careful. They are saying that you did not sign out."

Dumbfounded I replied, "Yes, I did."

He told me, "They are saying that you did not and they are going take your chair away the first chance they get."

In shock I asked, "Why?"

Steve said emphatically, "Just be careful!"

I got out of bed into my chair and went straight to the nurse's station and the log book to see what the complaint was about. Turning to the section marked for last names that start with D it was an easy find. Since I sign out every day at least once, my sheet was the first one after the divider. There it was plain as day, June 6 at 7:00 in the morning Jimmy Drew signed out of the building. I took a picture of it with my phone and placed the book back up on the counter and turned to find Steve. Physical therapy was at the other end of the hall and I am serious in that little old ladies with walkers passed me. Most of them were mumbling under their breath about me being so slow-poking down the hall. Steve had set my speed and I was going to abide by it if I wanted to keep the chair.

By the time I found Steve and got him back to the book to show him, that page had mysteriously disappeared. Then I went to Terri's office and said, "I know I signed out and even saw it there after y'all said I did not."

She said, "When Pat and I looked, we did not see it." I informed him "I took a very clear picture of it with my phone if you would like to see it." Her face fell like a worm dead apple dropping from the highest limb in the tree. Just at that moment Pat appeared at the door of Terri's office and handed me an envelope. The envelope had my name on it but was not sealed and was neatly folded inside was a thirty day notice to discharge for non-compliance. In other words, for not signing out. I looked up at her and asked, "Why are you doing this?'

Pat looked at me as if I were an infant child and said, "We worry about you."

I looked at her, then turned to Terri and said, "I signed out and I was going the speed that Steve set for me to go." Continuing I said, "My inside speed is one and I have not been off of that setting in the building." Then she told me, "It is not about your speed. You did not sign out." Making no mention of the picture I said, "I know that you know I signed out." Just then Terri said, "Jimmy, we have grown very fond of you and we are not trying to get rid of you." As Pat started to speak I felt like I was watching Venice and Serena volley at Wimbledon. She said, "I will rescind this letter if you sign out every time you leave."

Running low on patience I told her again, "I did sign out."

In a near admission she replied, "If something happens to you, this letter covers our backs." So that is what this was all about, and the reason they were scaring my psyche was over their fear of getting in trouble in the happenstance of me being involved in an accident. Even if I signed out every time I even thought about going somewhere I had no guarantee she would not uphold the letter.

My mission to bring the gospel of grace to hurting people was already receiving resistance. There was no one visiting me and the same pain that had driven me most of my life was tearing me inside out. My friends on Facebook were very supportive, but I was very lonely. With the random nature of a bouncing ball I began to think about places where I could go if I had to leave here. My first choice was finding a facility in Corpus Christi so I could be near Vance. I had already told him after the release of this book I would come down there to live. I wanted to get back to speaking in schools and Calallen High School would be a great place to start. I was sure of one thing with Vance: long before I reached the city limits of Corpus Christi everyone would know all about me. The first place I called I really liked the sound of, but they were private pay and my income would only cover about one week. I talked to this very nice man who gave me the phone number for the only facility in the area that accepted Nursing Home Medicaid. In what was an undisputable miracle, the one place in that area that would take me turned out to be the one place I would want to be.

The person that I spoke with in the administration office was named Norma. The main thing I wanted to know was what kind of equipment they had for me to exercise on. To my dismay they did not have a Nustep. There was a much more important reason to consider in my move than a place to workout. Vance had been talking about wanting me to come down and speak at an all school assembly. The greatest moments in my life have been when I was in front of a large audience sharing with them what God had done for me. It is an amazing and humbling experience to stand before hundreds of teenagers and have their undivided attention. I had one principal, Sam Chenowith, at Gladewater High School tell me he had never seen anyone come into a school and hold the kids' focus like I had. I walked onto a platform one night and faced hundreds of wound up, rowdy teenagers celebrating a lopsided victory and thought, *God, why did you do this to me.* Thirty seconds after I started speaking, their silence was freakish.

I knew that if I got moved into a facility in Corpus my old buddy who I had been down so many roads with could get me in front of a bunch of kids. I sent Amanda a text message and asked her if she knew where this place was. It had already worked to my great advantage that the only nursing home in Corpus that accepted Nursing Home Medicaid was in the Calallen School District. Amanda looked up the address and told me it was five miles from their house. That meant in my power chair I could get there in forty five minutes to an hour. So I began to wait and pray to see if Norma could get me approved. The only thing really worth staying for were my friends at Valero.

Sunday week before I left, I woke up having doubts about whether or not leaving here was God's will for me or just mine. There were people who lived here who did not have anyone but me in their lives. Joe had cried when I told him I was leaving and I wondered if I was being selfish. I sent Amy a message and asked her to pray with me for God to make it clear if he wanted me to go. I was not going to be able to go to church at Highland Terrace because it was raining so I went to the service they have at Greenville Health and Rehabilitation. That morning when I got up, my wallet was laying on my bed, and before I went to church I threw it in my drawer and locked it. By the time church was over, the rain had stopped and I went to get my wallet and go to the store.

I had just got my $60 dollar allowance and had spent $12 on a haircut the day before. The $48 that was supposed to be in my wallet was gone and there was my sign. The aides at night had stolen from me before and I had to be so careful about keeping valuables locked away. One girl who had been accused of stealing on my hall had not been terminated but just moved to another hall. Still I would wake up and find her in my room with my aide and suspected she had stolen from me. I approached my aide and told her not to bring her back into my room, but that night again woke to find them working my room. I sent Amy another message and asked her to pray for confirmation. The nurse on duty told the administrator but she never even asked me about it. I guess she was still mad at me for not signing out. I did tell Tanya there was no way to prove it was my night aide, even though I knew it was her.

The good thing about Steve's Valero on the corner was if I did not have money and wanted a refill it did not matter. I headed that way for solace with my friend Dianne. I filled my big super tanker jug with half sweet tea and half unsweet and told my friend what had happened. She got busy and I went outside to sit beside the store and watch the passing traffic on Business 69 and contemplate on what I was supposed to do. After only sitting there for a few seconds I heard the unmistakable sound of a Harley Davidson pull up. I looked to my right and saw a man who I did not recognize getting off the bike. After a few minutes I heard someone say, "Scooter Drew, you will love it in Corpus."

Then the man who had ridden up on the motorcycle said, "I saw on Facebook you were thinking about moving down there."

He knew I was having trouble placing him so he said, "I am Scott Welch." Scott had graduated two years before me and it had been over thirty years since I had seen him. Within thirty minutes of praying for confirmation, there it was almost a Daniel hand writing on the wall confirmation. He had gone in the store and asked Dianne if the guy in the wheelchair was Scooter Drew.

After I was approved, Vance borrowed a trailer from Coach Lamb to pull my chair on and he and Bryce came after me. I had them meet me at the store early Sunday morning so that I could spend a little last minute time with Dianne. My sweet friend had cried when she found out for sure I was leaving. We spent that night at Vance and Amanda's house but we located Trisun River Ridge first. It was not at all where they had thought it was and was not five miles from their house. My new temporary home was one mile from my friend's house. The next morning he had a summer workout to go to and then was coming home to get me checked in. I sent him a text message and told him I was going exploring.

Back to the facility was nine minutes from Vance because it was all uphill. There were no sidewalks, just wide shoulders on the busy street. On the way there I thought if Pat and Terri saw this they would both pass out. When I went inside and started meeting people, everyone was very warm and friendly and there was so much room. Vance had actually passed me on his way back to the house, smiling from ear to ear because he finally had me so close. I knew he was going after Sierra and he would be back with my stuff in just a few minutes. After Rosemary the receptionist finally located Norma, she came to greet me. An aide named Ashley helped me get everything squared away in my new room. We spent so much time talking and getting to know each other that a nurse poked her head in the room and said, "You do have other residents who need you."

Ashley gave me a big hug and said, "Do not go away. I will be right back."

She was Hispanic, so adorable with her dark complexion with dark hair with blonde highlights, and had seriously taken an interest in me. As I released her from our hug I told her, "I will wait forever if I have to."

After she had showed me my room, Vance and Sierra showed up with all of my things and helped me get unpacked. Before leaving he reminded me that practice started at eight in the morning in the field behind the field house. The next morning it was hard to wait on the sun to come up before leaving. As busy as traffic was on that street I did not relish the thought of riding in my power chair on the shoulder with cars speeding past a few feet away. It took seven minutes to get to the field house and there they were in all the heat and humidity of a Corpus summer morning and the first in line to run through the rope was Dakotta. I looked at Dakotta and Bryce as little brothers, and after being in Corpus for only one week I watched Dakotta and the rest of his power lifting team place first at the Junior Nationals Power Lifting Meet.

The weight room did not have anything for me to work on. The gym in the field house at Callallenm High School was what hard core lifters refer to as a Rocky Balboa Gym; all free weights, no air-conditioning and padded floors. I was so impressed with all the kids and it was easy to see why they consistently beat teams with much bigger players. In the fourth quarter when the big guys were sucking air with their hands on their knees between plays, the Wildcats were still fresh. I had developed such a bad case of tendonitis from working with free weights that I had spent six weeks in the hospital in Health South in Dallas.

On the way back to Trisun I stopped by Landshark Fitness to see if they had anything I could work with. The first lady I met was Susan who eagerly took me to the recumbent bicycle. She told me they would gladly get it moved to the outside for me so it would be easier to get on. Then it would be sitting next to a Schwinn Windjammer Arm Cycle, and thirty minutes on each gave me as good or better of a workout as a Nustep. I told her before I signed anything one of the Coaches would come by to work me a deal. Then she introduced me to the General Manger. I told Mckayla and her assistant Melody my story and that I had a book about my life in publication. The design team had just sent me an email with two options for the cover design and I showed her the one I chose. Mckayla took a picture of me and Melody and Susan and imposed an image of my book cover on it to go on their Facebook page. Mckayla generously gave me a free two month membership and asked if they could sell my book to members when it was released.

The next day I worked out early and then went to practice. After arriving at the field, I rolled up to Vance and told him, "Brother Susan worked me hard today."

Coach Hale looked at me with a big smile and said, "Are they treating you right there?"

I replied, "They are going to be of tremendous help."

About that time Coach Hartman walked up and asked me, "Why are you late?"

Me and Coach Hale looked at each other and smiled and then I told Coach Hartman, "I am going to be working out at Landshark Fitness and was getting used to everything this morning."

After practice that day I spent time with the legendary Coach Danaher. He will retire as the winningest coach in the history of Texas high school football and at any level. I always hate to shake a man's hand with my left hand, but Coach Danaher is a sensitive man and either from the stories Vance had told him he knew that my right hand was paralyzed and extended his left hand to me. Coach Danaher said, "Scooter, I have heard so much about you."

Humbly I replied, "Everyone knows who you are Coach Danaher. You are a legend."

He smiled softly as if I had embarrassed him and told me, "It is going to be good for our kids having a positive influence around."

Seeing my opportunity I said, "I am a great motivational speaker and I am at your service."

With that same soft smile he told me, "You are going to earn your keep, you are not going to roam the sidelines drinking up all the Gatorade for free."

That day when I got back to the facility I met the administrator for the first time. Liz had been off a few days and after we had introduced ourselves she said, "Jimmy, one of the employees said they saw you crossing the street."

With a horrible sinking feeling I said, "Yes, but I am very careful."

Thinking they were going to ground me I was delighted to hear her say, "Why don't you let our bus take you in the morning?" Then she added, "What time do you need to be there?"

Smiling like a small child who had just caught the Easter Bunny, I told her, "Fifteen minutes after six."

Liz asked me, "What time will we bring you back?"

In shock I asked, "And what about football practice?"

Softly she added, "They will take you there too." That was more important to me than working out because Coach Hale had told me I was not going to be a mascot or a fan. I was an honorary coach. Why else would Coach Danaher ask me for a play? We have a very legitimate shot at a state championship. This school has been to the playoffs twenty-eight years in a row, but this year's team will be powerful. Having me on the sideline will be like a ten point spot in every game. From the top athletes who never miss a play at their position to a third stringer who does not even play on special teams, my job is to make them feel like the most important person on the field. Now that is the gospel of grace and taking it to the most important people. Dakotta is the strongest kid on the team and a natural leader with our kids. When they see me take a big sweaty hug from him in the field house while we are lifting weights, it was not long before everyone was hugging me.

Monday through Thursday the bus picks me up at six fifteen and then from the gym takes me to football practice at eight. I am at all the practices and team meetings so that I can learn the offense. Coach Danaher said during the regular season when we have teams put away he may ask me for plays to call. I can be such a positive influence on those athletes. From the starters to the third stringers I love and encourage them all the same. God is giving me an entire high school to be a witness to and influence.

During the summer workouts, when only a relatively few of the team were there to participate, my bus would pick me up after practice and take me to the gym for my workout. I was worried about the toll it was going to take on me when we started our two-a-day workouts. One morning I was standing at the incline press in the weight room putting weight on my legs when Trevor Moses walked up and said, "Looking good Scoot." I told him, "It is frustrating since breaking my right leg I have so much nerve damage I bounce all over the place when I try to walk." Just then Kade Young walked up and overheard what I had said to Trevor. Kade asked me, "Have you tried to walk any lately?" My disappointment was apparent when I told him, "Yes at the rehab unit in Greenville I walked with a walker but we never went far because of the way my muscles would spasm." Trevor asked, "Coach Hale told us you walked before you broke your leg twice. Did you have muscles spasms then?" I said, "Not at all they told me it was due to nerve damage and it would go away as I got stronger." Then Kade replied, "Then let's get you stronger."

Every day after practice, with the help of at least three players we started walking. More than often it was more like twenty of them with one on each side of me supporting my arms and one following behind with my chair. Everyone else would just walk along offering encouragement and being supportive. By the time we started our two-a-day practices I knew that walking with them was much better exercise for me than anything at the gym. Coach Danaher sat down with me one day and gave me some good exercises to strengthen my core muscles. He told me, "When you develop your core you will hold yourself more upright when you walk and it will help you to pick up your bad leg."

Coach Danaher had the trainer put bands on my chair to use in doing crunches to strengthen me abdominal muscles.

Trevor's wife is a physical therapist and he has been a huge help. So while the team practices and then at night I exercise. Every day after practice I walk with the football players, Normally it is the same core group of guys insisting of Sean, Dakotta, Trevor, Kade, Tristan, Derek and Chase. They have been so good to work with me after their own grueling practices they shower and get back into their street clothes and come back out and work with me. Sometimes two hours after practice is over they are still out on the track with me.

Vance's son Dakotta was there with me whenever possible and his best buddy Blade was there every day. The first day we walked after practice was over 100 degrees with the Gulf Coast humidity. I walked forty yards that day with me sitting down for a few minutes every thirty feet. That day we made a goal for me to lead the team out onto the field at the state championship game and by week five for me to be able to walk one hundred yards. Before the start of regular season play I had walked one hundred yards in the sweltering Gulf Coast afternoon heat. By the time we had gone seventy yards I was panting like a hot dog and even Superstar was trying to get me to sit down. That day Trevor and Sean Vickers had my arms and there were parents filming us walking. Trevor's sister Heather was trying to hide her tears, but it moved me so much.

Something so special happened during two-a-days. I came down with the intention of motivating these young men and giving them the push they needed to overcome the size and athleticism of the teams they face in the finals to finally win a state championship. The kids fell in love with me and I fell in love with them. My job as motivation coach had turned inward and I was the motivated one. I want the state championship as badly as anyone. I want it for Coach Danaher and this community, as well as my kids. The harder I push myself, the harder this team pushes. By week two we were undefeated and I had walked two hundred and fifty yards. The spasticity that had inhibited me so badly while I was at Greenville Health And Rehabilitation was going away. It was so hard to get up and put weight on my legs with only a walker to support me. With those football players holding me up, I could just concentrate on walking and strengthen my legs.

Dakotta and Blade Bronstad, Trevor and Kade were good about coaching me as I walked. Telling me, "Stand up straight Scoot," or "Pick your right foot up Scoot." Everyone who walked with us would get involved. With the exception of Austin Revels. Austin and our other linebacker Sheldon Bammert were both selected to the All-South Texas team during their Junior year. We have arguably the best linebackers in the state and Austin is the hardest hitter of them all. He just does not say much. Even on the days where he was not hands on helping he just walks beside us smiling. I would say, "Austin you are in charge of motivating me." He would just look at me and smile and everyone knew that was all I was going to get out of him.

We rolled over our first three opponents but the fourth game of the year was called because of a lightning storm. It was not a district game it was just called no game. The week of that game, after the Wednesday practice I walked two hundred yards with the team. Sean "Dogfight": Vickers said, "Scoot you inspire us, the teams we play better be scared." He said that because now I had started walking on my own on the wheelchair ramp underneath the stands. The ramps wind around in three sections and are twenty five yards from top to bottom. They actually make perfect parallel bars and with the kids getting busy with school and focusing on the road to the finals, they were more than perfect for me to walk on my own. That day I had walked two hundred yards on the ramps by myself. Just two weeks earlier the first time I attempted to walk the twenty five yards from the bottom to the top, I fell down twice.

The next day I told the coaches what Dogfight had told me. Coach Danaher told the coaches they all had the week off next week because Scooter has the team inspired. Before the kickoff of the Carroll game, Coach Danaher told me I could no longer talk to players on the sidelines during the games. He had been worried about someone running out of bounds and getting hurt on my chair, so he regulated me to the track. Now even from the track I could not talk to them now though. I thought I was helping, but now I was told if I talked to any of the players I would be escorted off the field. During the summer they were all calling me coach and now I was not even Radio.

The next week was our first district game but it would be for district championship. Port Lavacka had beaten us two years in a row. With the team being focused on practice and school me getting to a place where I could walk on my own was a good thing. Without them holding me up the way they had, I would have never been able to get the strength back in my legs. I could no longer be on the sidelines or even on the field during pre-game. I took that to mean the practice field was off limit as well, so while they practiced I walked on the ramp. The Friday of our big game I went to the field early and started walking at noon. I sent Superstar and Kodak messages that I was going to walk 1000 yards for the team. I finished one hour before kick-off, but I walked 1000 yards totally on my own. I saw Kodak and Superstar in the fieldhouse and told them that I made it. That night we beat a team that had beaten us two years in a row 48 to 0. I sat at the back of the end zone and GQ and Sweetmeat had both ran over and handed me the ball after long touchdown runs. Kathleen Young and Tanya McDermitt told me it does not matter where you sit these boys love you and admire you. They reiterated they work harder for you and no matter what, I will be there for them.

The next week we had a bye and I could just focus on getting strong. Now that they had me to the point where I could just walk when I wanted, it was a lot easier. In that I did not have to depend on anyone else to help. Monday I walked 1200 hundred yards with the plan of building up to a mile by Friday. For some reason I woke up Tuesday morning and thought today I am walking a mile. I got to the stadium at noon and finished at 6:30. A broken neck, a head injury, eight weeks in a coma, bled to death, two broken legs and I walked a mile. The next day my hip was hurting and I fell down just before making it back to my chair. I lay there on the ground for a minute knowing help would soon be there. Dogfight asked, "Scoot are you alright?"

He was recovering from an ankle injury so I said, "You better yell and get some help." Sean looked up and laughing said, "Here comes the whole team." Just because I cannot talk to the players during the game does not mean I am any less part of this team. I sat at the back of the end zone during the Port Lavacka game because I knew if I were on the track the kids would talk to me. Then I would get escorted off the field and ran the risk of the warrants catching up with me. Coach Danaher had still asked me to come and be part of the team devotional. They will still load my power chair in the equipment truck for the out of town games. The big goal is a state championship and it does not matter where I sit or if I get to talk to the kids during the game. The only thing that matters is me blooming where I am planted and if I am called to be a rose garden at the back of the end zone, then that is what I will do.

Over and over I have found that if you will be thankful for your blessings in the hard times, God will bring you through anything no matter how hard it may be. No matter what life brings you, we must remember to bring to mind the things in our life that we are thankful for. While it is true that I cannot walk very well at this time, I can see and hear and against all odds I am walking again. One day curiosity got the best of me and I started experimenting with my chair. By tilting the seat all the way up and flipping the foot pedals up, I can hold onto the transfer handles and use my chair like a walker. Now while the team practices, I find someone to stand beside me and operate my chair and I circle the track with no one supporting me. It may not be pretty but I am ambulating and that is enough be thankful for in the darkest hour. Being thankful for my good eyes and ears makes more sense than crying over what my body cannot do. If I had not have faced all of the adversity that I have in my life, so many lives would not have been touched. I know if I had not turned to God when I came out of my coma, if I were still alive I would be laying in a hospital bed somewhere with a feeding tube down my nose.

Every single breath I take is something else to be grateful for. Every time my eyes open and see the light of day is another reason to thank God that I did not die while lost and spend eternity in hell. With every fall that I take, it is a reason to be thankful that I can still get to my feet. I broke my neck thirty years ago and am still fighting and exercising to walk again. I do not know why God never healed me totally, but I do not care. I am alive, and that is enough to be thankful for. We must always remember that God's ways are higher than ours and he always has a better plan for us than we could conceive on our own.

With each time that I failed in my life, I know that we serve a God that forgives. We are at the speed of light approaching prophetic times in which there will not be another chance to call out. Before you hit that rock wall with your head and wake up in the presence of demons, call on him to forgive you of your sins, and he will. It is a very simple thing that we do that gives us something we don't even have the right to ask for.

I am no angel, and the last person in the world to set himself above anyone. I have put my master back on the cross way to many times for that. Every choice that I have ever made in my life when recorded and summed has led me to a place in life where you do not want to be. I know what is like to be where the only thing you can do is scream out to God for another chance only to let him down again and again. As many mistakes as I have made in my life, I know that God does not make mistakes. He knew every misstep that I would take, and he even knew when.

The only way to recover from a bad choice or a string of bad choices is with good choices. When Isaiah said to wait on God, he did not mean to stop asking, nor did he mean to sit back and do nothing. When we wait on God, we are not giving up. We turn our back on the past and press on. The best way to forget about or get over your own problems is to help other people with theirs. It's not enough to just turn around; help someone else turn around.

My doctors tell me the average life span of a quadriplegic is eight years. I became a quadriplegic over thirty years ago. The last three years have been the hardest on me: sleeping in my truck, bathing in the bathroom sink at IHOP, and living on peanut butter. It is not that bad now, but I was there for two years. I waited for God though, and he moved in my life and consequently in the lives of others.

I had the great fortune of making the acquaintance of Zig Ziglar. Mr. Ziglar was a multi-best selling author and highly sought after speaker. After I came out of the coma and they moved me into a private room, someone brought me an old cassette recorder and a box of tapes. In with tapes by the Eagles, Van Morrison, and George Straight there was a motivational tape. Mr. Ziglar's voice was soothing to my troubled spirit and everything he said gave me hope. To everyone's surprise it was the only tape I wanted played. That tape made me believe that I could do anything and that all paralysis was to me was a temporary set back. If there ever was "a God thing," that tape being in that box was it.

After I moved to Oak Cliff, I started attending a bible study at Prestonwood Baptist Church. I knew that Zig attended there but I did not know he taught a Sunday school class. The class, which was always at capacity, was appropriately called the Encouragers. I went to there to meet him and tell him how he helped me through my midnight hour. A man in a greeter jacket told me Mr. Ziglar's daughter had passed away and he was in Nashville with his good friends, the Gaithers. The next week when I came back, the man that had done so much to encourage me was waiting for me at the door. I got to meet this man who had instilled in me such strong faith in myself and made such a big impact on my recovery. Mr. Ziglar is the one who taught me that it does not matter what happens to you; all that matters is what you do about it. He gave me hope and made me believe in myself for the first time in a long time. That day the Ziglar's took me took me to lunch after church and we got a good chance to talk. Mr. Ziglar told me, "Jimmy you really should write a book about your life." I asked him, "If I write a book will you write the forward?" In return he told me, "I would be honored to write the forward." Mr. Ziglar passed away before I could get my book published and that is why this book has no forward. That was going to be his honor and I could not give it to anyone else.

Prestonwood was a long drive from my house, and eventually I stopped going. Even though I never saw him, if I wrote him a letter, within a week I would have a personal reply. Paul, the music minister at Longview Metro, used his personal studio to make a CD for me to distribute to prospective youth pastors. I sent one to Mr. Ziglar and he told me that he would listen to it over and over. Mr. Ziglar saw something in me that most people did not see. He saw me as God sees me. He saw what God could do with me and what I could do with myself. That's the way I see people now that God's grace has made such a change in me.

This book is not about suffering. At the darkest point of your life, don't give up, or as Isaiah put it, wait on God. In the midnight hour when defeat has surrounded you and darkness engulfs you, do what Paul and Silas did in prison. The Bible says that in the midnight hour, they began singing praises to God, and their chains fell off of them, and a great earthquake opened the doors of the prison. The Apostle Paul said to give thanks in every situation especially when your back is against the wall. In the midnight hour, if you are digging into a jar of Peter Pan with your index finger for breakfast, lunch, and dinner, give thanks, and God will bring you through this.

Kade "IQ" Young, Coach Jimmy "Scooter" Drew

Sean "Dogfight" Vickers, Ricky "Babaloo"
Martinez (on the pipe)

Jimmy "Scooter" Drew, Dakotta "D Train" Hale`

Jimmy "Scooter" Drew and
Chase "Sweet Meat" Whetsel

Kade "IQ" Young, Jimmy "Scooter"
Drew, Austin "Bam" Revels

Trevor "Superstar" Moses, Jimmy "Scooter" Drew

Robert "Bulldog" Maldanado" Jimmy "Scooter"
Drew, Derek "Kodak" Scheible

Jimmy and the Winnsboro High School Cheerleaders.

Ricky "Babaloo" Martinez,
Jimmy "Scooter" Drew, Zach "Jugs" Roussell

John "Buff" Varnel and Jimmy "Scooter" Drew

my first scrimmage Rueben's dad was the field judge

Jimmy "Scooter" Drew and Conner "Touch Down" Lowrance

Jimmy and Holly

Jimmy and the kids at Macadonia Baptist.

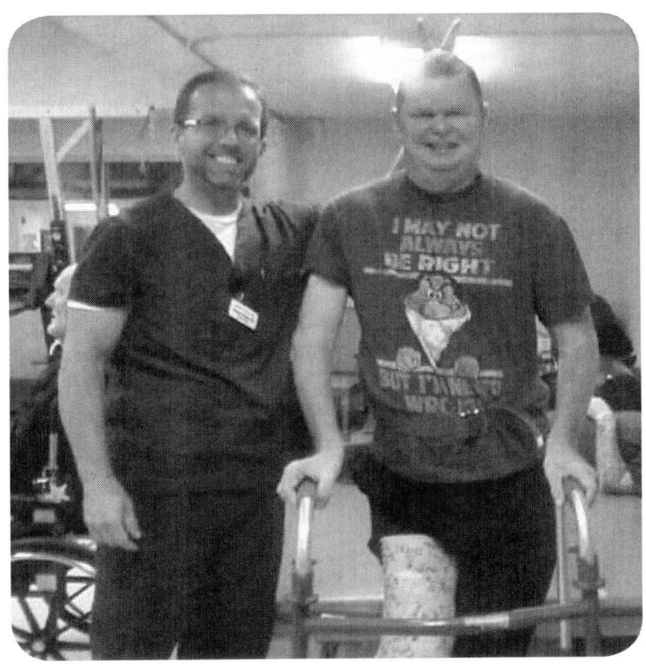

Helmut (physical therapist at Lengends), Jimmy Drew

Top Row: Dallas "7/11" Winterrod, Jared "Wild Man" Garcia,
Triston "GQ" Crossland, Jason Phillips, Treis Tagle
Bottom Row: Shawn Vickers, Jimmy "Scooter" Drew,
Derek "Kodak" Sheible, Ryan Taylor, Matt Vierra

My truck when I fell asleep and clipped the utility pole.

Chase "Sweet Meat" Whetsel, Trevor "Superstar" Moses,
in the back driving the chair Triston "GQ" Crossland
(look at the socks) Jimmy "Scooter" Drew, Derek "Kodak"
Scheible and Crieton "Captain Humility" McDermett

Blade "Switch Blade" Bronstadt, Jared "Wildman" Garcia,
Jimmy "Scooter" Drew and Chase "Sweetmeat" Whetsel
leaning forward going for speed

The first time I walked 100 yards

Walking with KK steering the chair and the
photo bombers are Ty and Race

Triston "GQ" Crossland hands Jimmy "Scooter"
Drew the ball after a long touch down run.